SPORT AND IDENTITY

by
Patsy Neal

DORRANCE & COMPANY
Philadelphia

DEDICATED TO:

Cary C. Boshamer

Whose love for physical education and sport has been shown through generous donation of interest, time, and money . . . and without whose encouragement this book couldn't have been published.

CONTENTS

PREFACE

My whole life has been involved in the sports world—just as my whole life has been involved in living. I think it is only right that at this point, I attempt to get away from the stagnant form of the orthodox textbook, and rather than give facts and techniques of performing physically, I attempt to give the flowing rhythm of a different type of physical experience—that which is blended with the life forces around us, and which comes from a few vital moments when the physical, mental, and emotional life is integrated into one finely tuned total life.

The thing I have tried to portray in this book is the importance of the *being* as it pertains to the sports world in particular, and to total life in general. I cannot separate the two, nor would I even if I could. For they are intertwined, and to pull one from the other would leave the individual without solidity or meaning. I know that I, myself, am not just an athlete; nor am I just a sojourner in life. I am a participant in athletics, *and* a participant in life. I could no more watch play going on around me without experiencing an active need to take part, than I could watch society revolving around me and feel no concern that I had been left out. Sports and life are—please pardon the expression—where it is all at. There is no separation—one leads into the other, and blends into an arena of agony and ecstasy, pain and pleasure, hope and discouragement, success and failures, and yes . . . happiness and unhappiness.

This is a textbook in the sense that it can be used in philosophy classes on the college level, and will be of help to teachers of physical education, coaches, athletes, physical education majors, and anyone interested in physical activity and the benefits of sports. It is also a textbook in the sense that out of my personal experiences, there has evolved a philosophy that can be digested and utilized on a classroom basis. However, this is not a textbook in the sense that its interest is limited to a classroom situation. Anyone who enjoys movement should enjoy reading this book. It also is not a textbook in the sense that these are proven facts. They are so to me . . . but as is true with any philosophy, there is no scientific way to run these thoughts through a computer and come out with proof as such. However, I believe that the millions participating in sports and competition testify to the fact that "something" is going on that is important to the individual, and it is my hope that I have touched on this "happening" in this book.

This book does not propose to give answers. There are some answers I will never find in my lifetime . . . nor would I want to, for some of the excitement of my profession is the seeking of new ideas and new sensations. I have simply tried to put down verbally what I personally believe should be the objectives of physical education and sports. I do this while knowing that some things do not lend themselves to verbal expression, nor are some objectives obtainable or some philosophies practical.

I do not attempt to follow any one school of thought, but have selected ideas that are applicable to what I feel as an individual . . . whether my philosophy deals with idealism, pragmatism, existentialism, realism, naturalism, or whatever is not nearly as important to me as whether my philosophy is valid and authentic.

At times, this book will be humorous and even happy. At other times, it will be serious and even sad. However, I hope that at no time will it appear indifferent. I have found it impossible to be indifferent in this world we live in today. We are living in times that could prove to be very tragic, while at the same time we are in a period that has all the makings of extreme excitement and achievement if we can just harness the power we have created with our minds. But there is more to our world than that which has been created by our mentality. At the edge of our achievements is a twilight zone that is relatively unexplored—that of the power of the human body when it has been integrated with the mind and the soul and the society it inhabits. It is this shading between the mental, the social, the spiritual, and the physical that this book is all about. It is what life is all about—and hopefully, it will help some individual to see what *he* is all about.

I have wanted to write this book for a long, long time . . . but it's not the type of book one would write without a lot of thought, or that one can write easily. I felt I had to write it now.

Brevard College   Patsy Neal

ACKNOWLEDGEMENTS

I always hesitate to attempt to acknowledge the many sources of help during the writing of a book because words seem so formal and inadequate. In some cases, it is impossible to single out individuals who have helped indirectly through encouragement, example, and sharing of thoughts.

However, there are many people who have made invaluable contributions toward the writing of this book. The administration of Brevard College, and the head of my department, "Chick" Martin, simplified the problem of insufficient time by allowing me to go to part-time teaching at Brevard College. Gail Anderson, a fellow teacher, has willingly done more than her share in helping me. And the Brevard College library staff, especially Mrs. Arline Campbell, Mrs. Mary Stevenson, and Mr. Charles Henrinski, have gone out of their way to make materials available to me. Other members of the administration and the faculty and staff of Brevard College have made me proud to be a part of a junior college setting.

I wish to thank Miss Dot Woodfin and Miss Carla Lowry for their many thought-provoking questions on varied subjects. Thanks also to Dr. Fran Koenig, who has helped me with research in many areas over the years.

Invaluable help with and contributions of photographs have been given by Bill Boggs, Jr., Joseph C. Bowles, Johnny Burr, Dave Chesnut, Kenton Deardorff, Pam Hill, Gary Kertz, Terry Muehr, Leo Purcell, Brona Roy, Richard Stevens, Howard Weir, Betty Westmoreland, and Dot Woodfin.

I am also thankful to Jo Ann Houts and the American Association for Health, Physical Education, and Recreation for permission to quote from Miss Houts's article, "Feeling and Perception in the Sport Experience."

At this time, I wish to thank Dr. Elizabeth Buie, Dr. Katherine Ley, Dr. O. N. Hunter, and Dr. Frances Schaafsma, who (probably unknowingly) have influenced my thinking and my philosophy—and whom I respect greatly for their contributions to our profession.

I am greatly indebted to the many students and professional people who have contributed to my life in so many wonderful ways. Special thanks to my family and friends who have given encouragement and shown patience during the endless writing hours.

No acknowledgement would be complete without thanking the many thousands who play and compete daily . . . and who made the writing of this book a pleasure.

INTRODUCTION

WHY PLAY? WHY COMPETE? WHY BE?

As long as I can remember, I have been an athlete. In bare feet I ran through the corn fields of Georgia in my childhood; threw clods of dirt over imaginary home plates, and knocked home runs with a tree limb and a rock. I was drawn to play as a bee to honey. There was something *there* that cruised through my blood and left me with moments of pure ecstasy . . . the running, the jumping, the throwing and catching . . . the mental and physical challenge.

These childhood games changed only in scope and organization. They became games with written rules. They became sports with known boundaries and specific penalties for infractions . . . with moments of drudgery and hard work sometimes replacing the pure ecstasy. The instantaneous spurts of movement in the morning sun or the evening twilight gave way to calculated planned practices, and the goals shifted from sticks and rocks to leather balls and expensive tennis rackets . . . but even so, after all these years . . . that spark of joy, that indescribable expression of being alive through movement has endured.

That same laughter that resulted from bouncing a tennis ball against the house and catching it, that same laughter that came from shooting balls through a makeshift basket while knowing a miss from certain angles would result in a water-soaked basketball in the family fishpond, as well as a water-soaked shooter from retrieving it . . . that same inward laughter that came from doing handstands in the hay barn has followed me to Mexico while playing in one-hundred-degree heat on outside courts, to Russia while playing in gigantic stadiums, and to the Pan-American Games and the World Tournament, and to thousands of other places. And the same floating, free, *oneness* feeling that has touched me while chasing hard-hit fly balls in bare feet

1

under a cloudless sky and with the breeze hitting my face has stayed with me and found me in intolerable siuations.

Have you ever felt *really* free while losing by twenty points in a crucial game, or while begging your legs to go one more time on the fast break because even though your body isn't willing, your mind and soul is? Have you ever felt *completely* sound at odd moments—even while enduring sore muscles, long hours of practice, the disappointments after months and years of preparation, the defeats on the court, and the solitary moments of doubt off the court. Well, I tell you . . . there *has* to be something there of real value to survive it all.

A question that has been thrown around in the physical education profession for many years is: Why does man play? Other questions that have been raised are those concerning whether there has to be a rational or logical reason why man plays or competes. Can we define why man engages in sport? Partially, I think . . . but not totally.

Is man motivated to run, to play, to exercise? Or does he *just* play? Does something *cause* him to play? Does he think "I need to run; therefore, I will run" . . . or does he just run? In some cases, man definitely does have *causality* for his physical activities. Many are jogging today because of the effect it has on the heart. Many students go through the motions of physical education because of the grade and the quality points needed for graduation. Many are going through strenuous exercise programs because of the great emphasis placed on physical fitness, or lack of it, in our culture today.

But what about the man or woman who plays *without* any known cause? Here is where we must go beyond the rational or logical element, and look at ourselves as *human* beings. In this situation, the individual is no longer ruled by his emotions and his thoughts. He does not *have* to have a reason. He plays; therefore, he plays. He runs; therefore, he runs. When man plays voluntarily, he no longer offers a simple answer to why he participates, or why he exists, or why he lives. He becomes a complex being . . . a *living* being . . . an individual that cannot be run through a computer and come out a number. He is *human*; therefore, he plays . . . he has legs; therefore, he runs . . . he is aware; therefore, he competes and responds because of the life forces that are his. And through awareness, the athlete responds to the spark that sport offers, because to do less would take away from the wholeness and happiness he seeks.

Often, I have asked myself what is it that has touched my life in such a personal way . . . that draws countless millions to participate in and to watch sports and athletics? Has every athlete felt what I have felt? Has every individual that has thrown a ball and hit a spike felt that intimate involvement . . . that inward laughter? I don't think so, for I have known athletes who apparently have played only for status, or for recognition, or for fulfillment of ego needs. I am sure that of the countless millions who compete, only a small percentage are *aware* of the lifeline that one can come into contact with, and that gives one a chance for *open* and boundless joy. There is no other word to describe it. It is joy in its purest sense . . . the fluidity of movement, the instant reactions under stress, the sense of control over body and mind, the creativeness of *being*. One is joyful because one is alive in the fullest sense. Why? Why there . . . in the sports world?

There are countless reasons why individuals enter into sport (some logical, some illogical . . . some caused, some without causality), but when the individual finds *meaning* in sports, then he has found *his* own, unique reason. But meaning has many connotations, and grows out of varied interests that depend greatly on the value system of the individual.

Some are interested only in financial returns. Joe Kapp says: "Winning is everything. You do anything you have to do to win. Everything else is crap." (121, p. 14) Other athletes seek the fame and success that comes from accomplishment in sports. Some seek a true self-concept. But regardless of the reason one enters into sports, usually the athlete's life or livelihood, except in extreme financial need, does not depend on his *doing* of sports. So if his life doesn't depend on the financial gain, the athlete finds himself or herself going beyond an interest . . . he becomes involved . . . and it is in this involvement he confronts himself.

Our culture has developed the concept that one plays for "fun." Consequently, we think of play as being an activity that

3

is pure leisure, and we do not give it any value beyond the pleasure.

Perhaps man intuits that play is somehow an irrational activity. He often plays for no good reason, yet he cannot, it seems, let himself live with this fact. Play becomes acceptable when man can explain his activity on rational grounds. The rational is superimposed upon the irrational. The absurd is made to conform to the reasonable. (110, p. 58).

If one plays only for fun, then one doesn't expect benefits from the activity as one does when one *works*. One works to make money in order to exist . . . or one works to make a living. Yet, if one recognizes that sport involves a combination of work *and* of play then one does expect the performer to show tangible results from the activity. In this case, one goes beyond the pleasure of the activity and channels his energies toward a particular *end*. As a result, one develops a goal based on work which allows the individual to at least *partly* enjoy what he is doing, and which is consistent with the concept of play and work set up by his society. Once one has a goal, one has to *work* to obtain it, just as one works in society to advance to a certain position. The higher the goal, the more culturally orientated sports becomes as it begins to take on a materialistic nature rather than an intrinsic one.

Spectators can identify with an activity directed toward a way of life they understand, such as: play better so you can make more money, win so you will be Number One, beat the others so you will have no competitive opposition. It is not easy to identify with a man's inner pleasure, nor with intrinsic goals that have no tangible products an onlooker can see and understand. So, as a result, our sports world has pushed the individual away from the joys of *inner* being and encourages him to go after the external values emphasized by our society.

We are fast losing the chance for fun within the sports world because so much emphasis is being placed on the product or the achievement, which comes only through *work*, rather than on individual pleasure, which comes through *play*. One finds sport

4

to be a creative venture on an intimate basis only when one participates in sports because of what sports *is* . . . not because of what sports can provide in our materialistic culture. But regardless of the motive, the athlete never experiences sports *only* as work or as play. One fringes upon the other. The excitement and the pleasure are there, sometimes at unexpected moments, just as the work and the drudgery are there. And even as he takes part, his participation is resulting in the creation of *something*, whether it is a moment of pure joy, or an opportunity to move into a higher financial bracket. He is as much an artist as the professional painter. He creates from what he is. What comes from his involvement in sports is a result of what type of person he *in reality* is. Perhaps this is what one speaks of when one speaks of an athlete as having the "spirit," or as being a "sport." One is a *sportsman* or not . . . it greatly depends upon the goals one seeks during the involvement.

But beyond the interest in playing, man becomes even more complex. He not only goes to play, but he goes to *compete*. Rarely does one enter into competition *wanting* to lose. But this does not necessarily mean that the athlete plays only to win either. Schollander says: "Once you get on top, there is terrific pressure to stay there. I'm not so much swimming to win now but not to lose." (181, p. 28)

But it is evident from watching sports in our society today, that many do play *only* to win: "Obviously the money counts, but to a pro there is the prestige of winning. You have a *personal* [italics mine] feeling of wanting to win." (21, pp. 16-17)

But if winning is the important thing, why do athletes and players keep coming back when they continually lose? Is there not something more . . . something that goes beyond a win . . . something that is not measured totally in the success of win-lost records?

There must be, and I know personally that there is, or only the winners would continue to play and to compete. Some reasons are easy to identify and have already been mentioned, such as status, fitness, ego-fulfilment, financial gain, etc. But what about the sand-lot players? What about the "pick-up" games? What about the games that arise spontaneously all over the land?

5

There *has* to be something more, or our success-orientated and commercially-geared society would have killed sports by now. Beyond the money, the status, the ego, the success, and all of the rest of the artificiality, there is a "happening."

What exists is opened to him in happenings, and what happens affects him as what is. Nothing is present for him except this one being, but it implicates the whole world. (29, p. 32)

What is this happening?

SPORT AND IDENTITY

PART I

A PHILOSOPHY OF PHYSICAL EDUCATION

Courtesy of Brevard College

THE SEARCH FOR MEANING THROUGH MOVEMENT

Educators through the years have tried to integrate the body and mind while instilling social values. Needless to say, we know almost as little about how one should go about this as our predecessors. Today, education in America is being disturbed by new values, trends, and social pressures. Every subject is having to explore its usefulness and its relevance in the educational curriculum.

Our problems are an outgrowth of the frustrations of *man*, and much of the upheaval we are facing now goes back to our inability to understand man and to give him a sense of unification and purposefulness as a total human being in the society he inhabits. We may never understand man fully, but until our explorations turn inward, we may never expect a happy universe, or even a happy neighborhood.

We may not come up with the vital answers we need tomorrow, or even in the next decade . . . but it's imperative that we start looking. Consequently, we can no longer be satisfied with stereotyped physical education programs any more than we can be satisfied with unworkable academic courses.

Many questions have been thrown out through the years regarding physical education, and the part it should play in the educational process.

How does one teach another to be emotionally mature? How does one teach the individual to have a realistic self-concept? How does one teach the student to get the most out of her unique body as far as movement and health are concerned? Is it enough to teach organic, neuromuscular, and interpretive knowledge? Is it possible to teach social and emotional responses in physical education, along with physical skills? Can one reach the mind in ways we have not thought of yet in order to more fully reach the body? Can one teach the body in ways that one can more effectively reach the powers of the mind?

How do I reach *him* or *her*? How do I separate the large

numbers of bodies into unique, single individuals with unique possibilities? How do I relate to the problems of the world through physical education? How do I contribute in a society that is focused on violence, drugs, and sex? How do I teach young people to turn on to their potentials without the use of artificial means and marijuana? How do I approach a personal teaching relationship that is workable for me, and beneficial to my students? How in heaven's name do I reach this world I live in . . . and more important, how do I reach the students I teach?

Do these questions bother you? They bother me. At times, I think I may have touched on one of the answers, just to find there is no verbal way to relay it through the teaching situation. At other times, I think I am on the threshold of understanding relationships only to find they are no longer applicable because of changing values and cultural standards. Sometimes, I have not even come close to a solution of any type . . . but there are other times when the processes of physical education have been so dynamic and so exciting that the answers have come automatically, creating in themselves even more stimulating problems. Frustrating? Sometimes. Thrilling? All the time.

One thing I do know . . . I *love* the simple feeling of being alive. I love to run. I love to breathe deeply after strenuous activity (is there a choice?). I love to feel tired if I have played well and long. I love to be able to take a problem and to work out the answers while going full speed. I love to be challenged, to have to respond in tough situations, to have to reach out a little to obtain things that are of value to me.

Another thing I know is that education, whether it is physical or academic, is not something isolated from my life and that I come in contact with only when I walk onto the campus and into the classroom. I am surrounded by education every minute of my life . . . and I revel in it. Thank God, I am alive . . . thank God, I can run . . . and jump . . . and feel, and think, and *be*. But how do I relate this sensation to my teaching? How do I instruct others so that they too can love life more fully? That they too can enjoy their ability to participate in life, and more specifically, how they can participate *happily* in physical activity?

12

These are not easy questions. I do not have the answers yet. I only want to offer some possibilities . . . how one applies them depends on one's teaching ability and one's own philosophy.

Opinions vary concerning the objectives of physical education. At least one educator feels that the organic, neuromuscular, and interpretive should be stressed more than the social and emotional values. (10, p. 24)

Another opinion is that physical education in the high school should work toward competence in chosen activities in order to prepare individuals for "their physical and recreational life." (10, p. 26)

Courtesy of Joseph C. Bowles

An interesting view is that given by Betty Lou Murphy (10, p. 27) who states that " . . . the proper focus of our field is not human movement but rather the study of sport. With sport as the focus, there may be possibilities for disciplinary development acceptance." She bases her opinion on two factors connected with sport: (1) sport can have meaning which allows the individual a chance for self-realization, and (2) sport has endured through the years, and is an "important social phenomenon of man."

Murphy goes on to point out that in order for meaning to occur, the individual must have sufficient skill to participate and that there must be intrinsic motivation for it to have a positive meaning. When one participates for reasons outside of the game itself—such as status, money, social influence, etc.— the game loses its real meaning. It is no longer *the* reason for playing.

Many other ideas have been expressed in articles and at conventions, along with the concern that physical education is not taking its rightful place, and sometimes is even being lost as a vital part of the curriculum, in our school systems.

For years, we as educators have proudly said that physical education *is* a vital part of education and that it integrates the whole body . . . but do we really believe it? We have fostered a spirit of isolation rather than integration in our teaching and our coaching. We train teams so that reactions are automatic and so they will work as smoothly oiled machines. We teach students to move in specific patterns that are stereotyped and which many times hold no meaning or naturalness for them as individuals. We teach specifics and generalities without encouraging our students to think through *why* or *how* . . . we teach physical skills and neglect vital psychological and sociological goals (the growing lack of sportsmanship is evidence of this). We go through calisthenics and exercises as though they were army drills (have you never wondered why there is so little laughter in physical education?).

No one has done more to isolate the body from the being than physical educators, and yet we wonder why physical education and sports take a back seat to other areas in order of importance. Yet, while physical education is taking its lumps from parents, students, other teachers, school boards, and the general public, the biggest drawing card in our society today is competive sports and recreational activities. Billions of dollars are being poured into recreation programs annually, and there seems to be no end to the growth of professional sports. So, in *spite* of us, recreational and sports activities have grown by leaps and bounds. Why?

In a world where money is a symbol of success, does it not seem a little strange that no college professor, college president, or Wall Street businessman can demand the salary of a Joe Namath or a Pete Maravich?

But what seems even stranger, is that while society as a whole is enjoying play activities and sports, the values placed on the *importance* of physical education and sports as a vital part of the educational process are almost nil. What is causing this discrepancy between society's interest and involvement, and society's value system?

> Perhaps . . . a similar hypothesis could account for the disdain with which intellectuals in general hold athletics and athletes. Perhaps the individual confidence, spirit of enterprise and independence nurtured on our playing fields constitute a threat to our current crop of social, economic, and philosophical planners. (228, p. 314)

Possibly, some of the ridicule aimed at athletes does stem from envy of those who can show physical and mental accomplishment, but the problem is much more complex. I personally believe that part of the problem is that we don't know enough about man as a moving, living being to give physical activity and sports their true place in our society. The total man is too complex, too unexplored—and this is what we witness in competition and in play—the complexity . . . the beauty of the unknown and untamed. We enjoy watching this mystery, but we don't know how to appreciate what we see because we don't understand it.

Another reason why lesser value is given to physical education and sports is because in the past the body has always been connected with the baser things of life. The Bible speaks often of the uncleanliness and the "sins" of the body, while most of our literature today deals with the body only in terms of sex, and sexuality, and weaknesses and handicaps of various types.

15

For some reason, authors do not write in terms of the poise, the balance, the coordination, the movement abilities, the many beauties of the body.

In people's minds, the body has always been connected with the "animal" part of man (does it not seem strange that most professional teams are named after animals? The Rams, the Bears, the Eagles, the Lions, etc. Isn't it also interesting that football names are usually connected with violent animals, while baseball teams have more refined and "uplifting" names such as the Cardinals, the Orioles, etc.? An interesting study would be an exploration of the given names of teams in particular sports, and their symbolic value). Even with our scientific advances, and our stress of importance on our world of today, our sports world is connected with another era. Even those that are not tagged from the animal world usually bear the label of another era of primitive life . . . the Vikings, Redskins, Chiefs, 49ers, etc. It is as though we ignore what man is today, and place him in a setting more appropriate to the agressiveness and physical action taking place on the field of action—or rather we place him in what we *think* should be the appropriate setting.

Man in earlier times competed for his life. He fought the wild animals around him, the elements that threatened him. Today, he in all appearances competes for status, for security, for business deals, and for victory . . . only his weapons differ. He is *still* competing for his life, but in a very different way. In earlier times, he had to protect his physical body from real physical danger. Today, he seeks to protect his life by maintaining his self-concept, or his "ego." But regardless of the connotation, the individual still seeks to save *himself*. His life is tied up in the value he places on the self, which includes the physical self regardless of how one views it, for without it there *is* no life on this earth as we know it. For one cannot save the soul or the mind without saving the body . . . there is no separation *here*.

Realizing this, one must realize the importance of the body. The truth is that we have been *conditioned* through the years to think of the body as an inferior part of the individual. Is it not possible that it is not inferior to the mind and the soul while here on earth? Is it not highly likely that the dignity of man may be *in* the body—in his ability to control it? Is it not

16

possible that this is why millions flock to sporting events . . . because they witness this struggle for dignity through perfection and self-control of the *total* man? This is the thought I want to explore, because this is what I believe.

Contrary to what our educational systems indicate, education doesn't start in school. It starts when the baby is born, and continues as he learns through *physical* exploration—he touches the fingers to the face; his toes go to his mouth; then one day he crawls, and then he tottles, and soon he walks, and then finally he runs—all accomplishments of the *body*, or more specifically of what he contains as a unit in the body . . . the mind, the neurological processes, etc. And when do we start to separate this working unit that has accomplished so much on its own and through cooperative effort? Yep . . . in school. We teach him math, and then he stops learning math so he can learn English, and then . . . well, the only fun spot in this educational process at the lower levels is the *play* period. Then he becomes a *whole* person again. It is *he* that runs, and jumps, and shouts, and thinks, and does.

But educators that we are, we even ruin this aspect of education in later years. Physical education is no longer *fun*, is no longer a *wholeness* experience . . . and consequently, no longer a vital educational process. It becomes drills, and work, and grading, and dullness. It becomes *forced doing*, when what the individual wants and needs is *expressive being*.

In the profession of physical education, there is the uniqueness of *total* involvement and the chance for meaning. Eleanor Metheny has expressed this so well:

> . . . *kinesthetic perception of movement* is one of the sources from which man derives the *meanings* of his life as he carries on the uniquely *human mental process of transforming sensory perception* into human thought. (129, p. 114)

Yet, these meanings in sport have been shaded by a thousand different influences being exerted by our success-oriented society. Even the language reflects this division of meaning as we look at some of the terms used in play activities and sports

17

such as "playing for," "playing with," "playing against," etc. We play *for* victory in sports; we play *for* grades in physical education. We play *against* in professional sports; we play *with* in physical education. We play *for real* in athletics; we play *for fun* in gym. We *work* hard in intercollegiate sports; we *play* hard in our classes.

Do you not wonder what is going on in two related areas when even the terminology is so different? Evidently, it is the goals and the objectives that make the two areas of physical education and athletics so different, but *should* they differ? Or if so, should they differ so greatly? Is it not possible that the same process is going on in each, but simply at a different skill level? Or is it not possible it *would* be going on if we did not force the process into other channels because of the stress on winning?

It is usually accepted that "play" is a voluntary activity, that "games" are recreational activity which have rules and usually involves some type of competition between two or more people or groups, and that "sport" is organized competition with formal coaching and instruction, and results in leagues, championships, etc.

Although this chapter deals with a philosophy of physical education, which by all logical standards should come under the terminology of "play" and "games," I personally feel that "sport" is also a very vital part *as defined here*, not as defined by our culture which has placed almost total value on the winning process. Therefore, for clarification purposes, I wish to define "sport" as organized competition which results in testing on a high level of skill filled with pressure-producing situations, while "play" and "games" is testing of the individual on a lower level of skill with fewer pressures. With this definition, the processes going on in "play," "games," and "sport" are interchangeable and differ only in degree and situational background.

So just what is this process? And how does it relate to physical education and sports?

In referring to games handed down over the years and which have become "permanent" in the folklore of children's games, Phillips (162, p. 66) proposes the following theory:

18

(1) Through group activity, children try to master anxieties connected to specific life situations.
(2) Anxiety is lessened through symbolic acts during the game.
(3) The meaning of games is unconsciously understood by adults and children.
(4) A child voluntarily quits playing a specific game when he has "mastered his anxiety regarding the related life experiences."

Erikson says:

> The playing adult steps sideward into another reality; the playing child advances forward to new steps of mastery. I propose the theory that the child's play is the infantile form of the human ability to deal with experience by creating model situations and to master reality by experiment and planning. (57, pp. 212-222)

Caillois (30) feels that the freedom of play allows the individual to develop "in a separate, ideal world, sheltered from any fatal consequences."

There is no simple answer to why man plays, but at least part of our fascination with play, sports, and competition seems to be our attempt to touch on life without getting fatally burned by going near the fire. In other words, sports allow us to come into contact with life as we would like it to be if we dared take the chance *for real*. We *play* at being firemen and policemen. We *play* at being professional quarterbacks on the sandlots, and shutout pitchers in physical education classes. We *play* at being daring and brave and strong in game situations. We *play at it* because *it's not for real* . . . yet, inside of us we *wished* it were. How often have you heard the comment: "Boy, if I could just do that every time"? "If I could hit tomorrow like I'm hitting today, no one could stop me." "If I could just do what I'm capable of doing, everything would be all right."

If?

In games, we allow ourselves to say "why not?" For in play and in games, one has the opportunity to test oneself without losing anything, or having anything of great value at stake.

But as one moves up the scale of skill, and goes from play to games to sports, or from physical education to intercollegiates and professional sports, there *is* more and more at stake. Why? Because the thing that is really at stake in our play situations is the *self* . . . our self-concept . . . or the mastery of the self.

The saving value is that when one's self-concept is too threatened, one can withdraw at any time from play or a game: "I don't want to play any more." One can also withdraw from the sport situation, even though it is harder to explain if one is still capable of playing well. However, one can't withdraw from life short of suicide or some extreme psychological change.

As one becomes more and more involved, and more and more experienced, one presses harder to do well. Sometimes, the play becomes so intense that we must continually remind ourselves it is *only* a game . . . but is it? The men working under Vince Lombardi didn't think so. The men who "retire" from professional sport because they no longer enjoy it don't think so. But for all purposes, as viewed by our society, it *is* still a game because one can withdraw from it without any real permanent damange to the self, and without any vital loss of prestige or status in our society.

Does it seem so strange that we watch *plays* on stage, and that we watch athletes *play* at sports? They both are performances. They both have actors *playing* at the real thing, and trying to become involved to such a degree that their actions become perfected and authentic. Players "suit up" for their performances, while actors "dress up." Players nor actors "suit up" or "dress up" for practice because it's not the *real thing*. Everyone plays his role, but what part is a role, and what part is real?

Performances on the stage and on the field signify a *need* in man. The question is: what need do play and sport fulfill in man that he does not find easily in life?

The answer to me is simple. He seeks *meaning*, and the only way to attain it is to test himself to see what is *there*. In play, he can take himself to the outermost and uttermost limits, and the findings and the efforts are rarely ever fatal. One opens oneself to the environment and to his *being* . . . one tests his environment and his being . . . and one conquers it or one

20

doesn't . . . but the absolute thrill comes in the confrontation and the discovery, even though it may be painful and even agony. And the beautiful thing is that *one can always come back to play another day*. Defeat is a temporary thing . . . not permanent as it sometimes is in life.

Play is risk, challenge, creativeness, fantasy, self-discipline, caring, involvement, and a thousand other things all tied up in *total being*. "The Thou confronts me. But I step into direct relation with it. Hence the relation means being chosen and choosing, suffering and action in one . . . " (29, p. 76)

Courtesy of Brevard College. Richard Stevens, Photographer.

Sport has remained an attraction to thousands and millions because it exemplifies man's search for perfection . . . it shows man's accomplishments and defeats . . . it allows glimpses of what man is, but also of what he *could* be. The Babe Ruths, the Arnold Palmers, the Babe Zahariases . . . they were in sport what many men want to be in life . . . fearless and bold, calm though afraid, winners and losers but always dignified competi-

21

tors, intense and joyful, weary but brave . . . quiet but sometimes obnoxious . . . but most of all, superhuman *but human*. They pointed to the god in us all if we but dared to set it free . . . those heroes we watch Sunday after Sunday are *us* . . . they are what we want to be *ourselves* . . . they are *in it*, and we envy them enough to watch them and boo them, and we love their daring enough to even cheer them in their moments of glory.

Is there any wonder that sports expand as man becomes more and more disgusted with the universe in which he lives? He seeks meaning to who and what he is . . . and he proves its authenticity by seeking it under pressure.

Life is disequilibrium. Stillness is death . . . We seek disequilibrium in action and in repose, in soaring and cycling, in booze and pot . . . In no other thing is disequilibrium so perfectly embodied as in the ball—and around no other object has man fashioned so many games . . . (219, pp. 63-64)

Courtesy of Brevard College. Kenton Deardorff, Photographer.

In play and in sport, it is the *now* we involve ourselves in—it is the action of the moment we relish. In sport and in physical activity, we seek who and what we are because to do less would mean to be less. Man is a changing, moving, living, being whom we do not really know, but whom we seek all our days in any way we can without losing ourselves in the process. And when man finds a way to confront himself, he absorbs fantastic amounts of pain to stay in contact with that he seeks. "Life is not a stable state, but a rhythm, an alternation, a succession of new births." (217, p. 218)

Why does man play? Perhaps because we must "play the game" to get the benefits out of playing the game. Meaning isn't solely in perfecting skills, but it is the *taking part*—in pitting yourself against others and against the environment—the improvement of physical skills comes as one plays . . . and so does self-awareness.

Vince Lombardi showed this need to take part when he explained he wasn't accepting the Washington Redskin coaching job because of the money ($100,000 salary and $500,000 of Redskin stock). "I don't need the money. Money I've got. I need to *coach!*" (93, p. 29)

And *we need to play and to compete.* "Athletes make their bodies do things, accomplish things—extraordinary things—and endure the pain." (228, p. 311)

We need to play and to compete because we need to know who we are, and it is in play activities we come the closest to discovering ourselves.

According to Jean-Paul Sartre, man invents himself, he designs his own "essence"; that is to say, what he essentially is, including what he should be, or ought to become. However, I think the meaning of our existence is not invented by ourselves, but rather detected. (61, p. 157)

We find meaning in play and in sports because we dare detect things about ourselves we would not dare in real life. We find meaning because there is *something* there. There is a vital "happening" in play activities. There is an *involvement* . . . the being is there, *and in the thereness, there is the being.*

Physical activity is an expression of what is going on *inside* an

23

individual, as well as *outside* the individual. When I develop the skill to put the basketball through the basket, I am developing *more* than an isolated skill. I'm developing the ability to *do something*. I have taken an impersonal object and accomplished a specific goal through self-mastery of space, time, and movement. And if a person can "do something" he intends to do through control of the self, whether it is a physical "happening" or otherwise—then it *is* meaningful.

Therefore, my philosophy of physical education is that movement should serve as an educational experience for the *whole* body. Total life should be the vital concern of every individual, and the ability to help students relate more adequately and more abundantly to the life around him or her should be the main objective of the educator. Education that is not usable is as bad as illiteracy. Neither helps the individual. One facet simply stagnates, while the other never materializes. We are *living, moving, thinking, feeling, seeking organisms*, and to try to educate one part of the individual while ignoring the other parts, is a defeating and ridiculous goal. It is through the sensory perception experienced during movement that we have the chance to become aware of ourselves . . . to touch on a self-concept within a world of many variables.

We can educate the man or the woman *within* the physical, and should make every effort to do so . . . but we cannot educate *only* the physical. Education involves the *whole* body and the *whole* being . . . understanding this fact would make a difference in our approach to physical education. Over a period of time, we might even restore the laughter and the fun to physical education and to sports.

If ever physical education is to become a vital part of the educational process, we must use movement to open up avenues for increased self-awareness, greater sensitivity to the needs of others as well as to our own needs, more expressive creativeness, self-discipline, coordination, balance, rhythm, increased efficiency of the body to respond and to adjust—and a feeling of beauty in the integration of the body with the mind, soul, and external environment.

Everything revolves around the individual. Every decision we make affects *us*. Everything we do is centered in *our* desires and

24

Courtesy of Clear Creek High School

our goals. To appreciate our lives, we must become acquainted with the core of the being ... with the self. "Beyond the psychoanalytic frame of reference, there appears the search for the ineffable "it"—the wild, divine, mysterious, beautiful force of life itself— ... " (201, p. 555)

Believing that sport is just an extension of physical education, where the process of self-discovery is taking place at a higher level of skill and under more pressure, I will explore this process in greater detail in the section on sports and competition.

PART II

A PHILOSOPHY OF SPORT AND COMPETITION

Courtesy of Clear Creek High School. John Burr, Photographer.

Chapter 1

FREEDOM AND LIMITATIONS OF SPORTS

As everyone knows, sports place limits on the individual. Rules limit the violence and the means one can "legally" use to obtain specific goals. Space limits the extent of the movement, such as floor space in free exercise and the approach area in bowling. Time limits the opportunity for extensive emotional and physical concentration on obtaining a goal, as there are time-outs between plays, quarters, halves, etc. Force even is limited, as one cannot use "unnecessary roughness," or cannot "hold." As the athlete participates under the many limitations imposed upon him by his particular sport, he becomes aware that all things have certain boundaries of limitations, even life.

At the same time, the *meaning* an athlete can derive from the sports situation is not limited. The depth present for knowing oneself is unlimited and almost unknown. Within the boundaries of the sports world, the athlete can develop all of his or her potential, and become a meaningful part of the world he lives in . . . or he can choose to remain closed to his potential, and never experience his personhood completely.

When the individual finds within sports a sense of "being," or a reason why he feels fully alive during participation, then he begins to experience a real sense of freedom. This freedom deals with life forces beyond the rules of the game and allows an expression of openness and *aliveness*. This "being" becomes a thing of awareness which evolves to an understanding and a clarification of self. As Don Schollander put it,

> . . . Before you decide how you want to live your life, you must look at yourself and *attempt* to know yourself. I look at myself as a person who's trying to develop as an individual. It's been important to me throughout my life to be much more than a student, to be much more than an

athlete, to be much more than *anything*. (181, p. 26)

The individual becomes free to *exist* . . . not in a haphazard or coincidental way, but eagerly. He begins to know his body. And as he becomes acquainted with his body, he gains a broader realization of self, again freeing himself to learn more about who and what he is.

In the sports realm, the athlete learns to relate his total being to circumstances around him. He loses himself in sports while at the same time finding himself. Most athletes do not see sports as an arena of escape from emotional tension, aggressions, etc, but as an open space within which they can work to achieve specific goals through physical expression. Consciously, or subconsciously, they build toward a self that holds meaning to them as individuals. Even with the limitations of the rules, the athlete has the chance to gain freedom for himself because in his involvement he must make meaningful choices if he is to cope with the many pressures he is faced with. He is faced with the challenge to "live by the rules," just as all players are, while at the same time he has the chance to formulate his own rules according to the validity of his identity and how he relates with others and the world around him.

It is evident that choice is not completely "free" in sports. Some things are definitely defined by rules and regulations. Yet, there are other areas where one undoubtedly has a choice of how one would react, without being determined by rules of the game; thereby, the responsibility is placed upon the athlete for his or her actions.

In order to understand modes of meaning particularly or singularly related to the sport experience, perhaps we need to examine the structure that gives meaning to sport. One way to view structure is to conceive of it as freeing the individual rather than restraining him. The fewer the variables or alternatives which are *not* prescribed, the greater the freedom the individual has within those alternatives. (59, p. 44)

When there are alternatives for action (such as we find within the "spirit" of the rules), then man must make decisions as to what is the *best* thing to do, or the *right* thing as far as a response. Confronted with a freedom of choice, he must accept responsibility for any decisions he makes which affect him as an individual—either physically, or mentally and morally if he is to receive full benefits from his actions. Most situations during competition do not allow for mental contemplation. Choices are made on the basis of what works, or what doesn't work. The basketball player drives to the right of the defending player because this has proven to be a weak point. The badminton player hits a deep clear and then uses a drop shot because it gets points when done effectively. But then there are choices that go beyond the practicability of performing effectively. One chooses to admit that one touched the ball last before it went out of bounds because one *did*.

Freedom of choice in sports is necessary for self-revelation. The athlete finds out who he is through the choices he makes. Man reconfirms his own identity within the framework of the rules, and finds *his* own truth by his decisions. The more rules, and the more limited the framework of free choice, the less personal development and creativity one has the chance to achieve. "In sport, challenge is defined and perceivable. It is related to the areas of freedom; that is, whereas many variables are held constant, both freedom and challenge exist in relation to those variables which are not held constant." (59, p. 44)

Man doesn't have to "live up" to things when he is free, for he *is*. His being is what he is aware of . . . and he has no need to seek more or to prove it. True freedom only comes with responsibility, for one is responsible for what one is and for what one *does* with what one is.

The individual carries his own values into sports. What one is *aware* of determines what decisions one makes. Some are aware of codes of conduct that others are not. Some place value where others do not. Decisions become a *personal* thing, based on what one *really* is . . . and this is where the action is. This is where one really finds out how good he is—not only physically, but emotionally.

All players have the same rules . . . yet, each individual reacts differently, and each individual performs differently, for there

31

is *more* than the rules for each player. There is the *way* he or she is involved. There are the emotions he or she *feels*. There are the decisions he or she *makes*. And above all, there is *his* or *her* performance. It is the performance, the real acting out, or the total being that is the key to why so many engage in sports. It is here that one finds expressions of existence, of personal identity. One leaves the limbo of rules set up for everybody and enters an unlimited field of *personal* potential and being. One expresses what one is through one's *actions*.

Courtesy of Brevard College. Bill Boggs, Photographer.

As one competes, one finds that one can be *free from* certain things . . . and that one can be *free to do* other things. The individual no longer embraces indifference and uninvolvement. The athlete must open up to what is there or lose what he or she is. Perhaps this is what Lance Alworth was feeling when he ended his retirement from professional football with this statement: "I couldn't stand watching the game. I wanted to be part of it." (7, p. 1B)

32

One can find an immensely satisfying freedom from the self as one participates in sport. One rides the waves and forgets everything but the attempt to maintain balance and rhythm with the water. One becomes "caught up" in the action of the fast break and forgets everything but the joy of the movement and the potential of the moment for an achievement that is personal, and yet is not personal. It is as though one transcends himself and enters another world where there is something bigger and better than man himself. For small precious moments, one enters paradise.

Value Structure in Sport

Each phase of sport has its own value. Each time a man jumps, or runs, or throws, there is meaning of some kind to the individual, either conscious or unconscious. This movement becomes more significant to the discovery of self, as it becomes more meaningful.

Within the value system of sport, rules determine what happens to a certain extent, as they regulate what is legal and illegal, what will be rewarded and what will be punished, and in a sense, what will be accomplished and what will not.

To fully understand the value of sport, each individual must be aware that values evolve around man, around man's ability to choose, and around man's awareness of a hierarchy of worth; therefore, the concern must be with man himself, rather than with what he can produce through specialized technique and mechanization.

Sports, as being pushed in our culture today, have superficial goals based on superficial values. Realities are lost in the ever-present pressures to *win*. Philipp D. Woolpert, who went from big time coaching at the University of San Francisco to a job with less pressure on winning, made this comment: "This may be heresy, but I think there is something wrong with these games we play when winning becomes a motivating factor of behavior beyond the game itself . . . We have come to believe the only real measure of accomplishment comes in victory. It's the product of a bad system of values. Hell, it creates psychological problems where there shouldn't be any." (95, p. 68)

Man, especially the athlete, escapes from looking at himself by focusing on victory as *the* goal. Most of us never dare look for a purpose over and above victory. This is shown every day in our desire to dominate things around us. We *kill* birds. We *catch* fish. We *tame* wild animals. We *conquer* Mt. Everest. We *beat* others in bridge and bowling, and whatever. We "wipe out" our opponents on the basketball court. We continually consider ourselves to be winners when we exhibit enough power or skill to exert control over other things or other beings. Jim Marshall said, "This is a punishing game and you have to punish people if you want to win. You have to hit people. That's what you have to do. Not intimidate people. Dominate. You have to dominate them." (121, p. 16) What kind of people are we?

Courtesy of Clear Creek High School. John Burr, Photographer.

Is it we seek meaning in *action* rather than in *being?* Perhaps our obsessions with violence and killing and defeating are our inept way of seeking *some* goal to give life meaning. In our world of competition and violence, perhaps these forms of action are the only thing that seems real and of value to us as individuals.

> . . . so many people judge the value of their actions not on the basis of the action itself, but on the basis of how the action is accepted. It is as though one had always to postpone his judgment until he looked at his audience The person who is passive, to whom or for whom the act is done, has the power to make the act effective or ineffective, rather than the one who is doing it. Thus we tend to be *performers* in life rather than persons who live and act as selves. (123, p. 53)

Seeking something in such opposition to what is ordinarily accepted by our society probably seems absurd . . . but to chase something without meaning is just as absurd, or more so. We seek meaning in our value, and when it is not there we revolt or we turn elsewhere. We march on Washington; we have moratoriums; we turn to LSD. The athlete also seeks meaning in his values. And if these values are patterned after those of the culture, he is tuned in to those things so many people are finding lacking today, and even the athlete becomes disillusioned— as evidenced by the troubles coaches are having today in big-time athletics.

If one has values *without* meaning, one finds himself holding to a sense of nothingness. Fred Van Dyke put it this way:

> Guys ride big waves for ego support, to compensate for something that is lacking in their lives . . . They have an underlying feeling that they're not doing anything with meaning. Man needs an outlet that's ego-gratifying. Surfing gives you a feeling of accomplishment. But the feeling's gone in four seconds, and then you have to start all over again.
>
> Surfing should be fun. It's not fun. It's absolute terror. Big-wave riders are scared people. They have to go out there to prove they're not afraid, to prove their masculinity . . . Once I broke my board in half . . . I knew I hit the ultimate . . . Then I realized what a complete farce it was. I

35

still surf, because I'm a victim of my culture. I can't transcend it. (180, p. 104)

No one has a meaningful life *tomorrow* if the values he seeks *today* have no meaning. *One's values must have meaning now.* This is why the sports involvement must be real if there is to be meaning. But the involvement is not a future possibility . . . it has possibility only if utilized *now* . . . today . . . at this moment. This is the beauty in sport. The individual is caught up in the action of the moment. He is totally involved in the present and his being has existence at that point in time. *He is there,* and as such he is *meeting* meaning by his thereness. The athlete doesn't think in terms of *after* the game while playing. He thinks in terms of *during* the game, for his involvement is not a future thing, but a thing of the present. That second is his reality, and as such he chooses to live it at that time. So to those who are aware, *the value is in the total participation of the being,* not in the results. And as such, the value and the meaning are the same.

The sad thing about most of our competitive programs is that many athletes do not realize there is more to the game than the value of winning and losing. John Vallely said, "People still ask about the challenge of playing without Lew and about the pressure of winning. I've never really thought of it in terms of pressure. Not winning just has never occurred to me. We've always been winners here, all of us from high school on. Winning is the only thing we know. There are no other options." (102, p. 9) Athletes who have thought only in terms of winning have at least given some meaning to their competition by wanting to win. If these athletes didn't have victory as their goal, for many there would be no meaning of any kind, and consequently, *nothingness* in their participation.

Depending on what one wishes to attain, one can become very frustrated in sport. To know when you have achieved, you must have some type of a value structure. To know when you have a meaningful life, you must also have some idea of what a meaningful life is. If one is concerned only with scoring, and one misses the basket, then as far as the individual is concerned, he has failed completely. *Everything* he has aimed for was tied up in his ability to hit a thing a few inches in diameter. The fact that he came close does not count. The fact that the ball rolled around the rim and then fell away does not count. If the ball doesn't go into the basket then he doesn't get the points. So, if one's value structure is built around physical achievements measured in inches and seconds, one finds that one fails more than one succeeds. "I almost made it" has no value. But if a man's value structure is built around things that go beyond the scoreboard and the ability to attain practical ends, then the

Courtesy of Clear Creek High School. John Burr, Photographer.

athlete can find meaning in the movement itself regardless of the final placement of the ball. "It felt good when I released it" has a different meaning than "It almost went in." One becomes aware of *more* than the end result. There is the actual involvement of the muscles and the mind during the attempt . . . and nothing can take away from this feeling of integration. The

37

individual *performs* with a feeling of pride even if he doesn't score. "Useless? Why, it cannot ever be useless. To perform is to live, and everything else is waiting," said Karl Wallenda. (109, p. 21) The athlete can still experience a feeling of success in the fact that the form was good, and there was that moment of exhilaration as the body was suspended in the air. The movement itself was a *joy*, even though the end was not fully obtained.

Freedom of Choice and Will

When we talk of value structures, we must recognize that value for the individual can only exist where there is a choice and a freedom to choose. What the athlete becomes is dependent upon his choices. He moulds his own life according to what he chooses to be through his actions. Freedom of choice is a necessity if one is to "become." Where there is limited freedom, there is also limited fulfilment. "It is, in part, the *choice* that brings about self-realization." (202, p. 56) If the coach makes all the decisions, then the athlete has lost his right to share in the blame, or in the glory, since the responsibility for his actions is no longer his, and consequently, he loses his potential as a free man by default.

Man becomes through internal choices, not through external rules. True, rules, just as laws, can make a man conscious of certain facts and truths, and in this way can possibly lead him to incorporate these laws within himself as internalized rules. However, the power is *in* the man, not in the outer alternatives.

The one is the soul's becoming a unity. That is something that takes place not between man and God, but in man. Power is concentrated, everything that tries to divert it is drawn into the orbit of its mastery, the being is alone in itself and rejoices, as Paracelsus says, in its exaltation. This is the decisive moment for a man. Without it he is unfit for the work of the spirit; with it, he decides, in his innermost being, if this means a breathing-space, or the sufficient end of his way. (29, p. 86)

38

Man must face the *now* . . . and in the confrontation, he faces the alternatives and consequences present in *the* moment, and based on what is valuable to him, he must choose, and be. To narrow the choices externally is to deny the full potential of the moment. Once a man finds his choices made for him, he finds the responsibility for his being and his actions also shifted. He no longer bears the burden for what he would choose . . . therefore, he does not really become what he is *completely*.

Sport and philosophy are similar. In each, it is the individual's responsibility to define the terms and the rules of his own existence as a human being. He is free to choose, but he must be aware that with his freedom comes responsibility. One does not negate consequences through choice. One accepts them as being part of the price for attaining something of worth.

The athlete cannot change most things he is involved with in competition. He certainly cannot change what has been predetermined by rules he must play by. The tennis ball is a certain dimension and the net is so high. He has a certain amount of space he can hit into and no more without hitting the ball out-of-bounds. Where these unchangeables are concerned, the best he can hope to do is to relate to what is there. He does this by his choices and his actions. He hits the ball so high to clear the net. He chooses to hit the ball within the boundary lines when possible. He chases the ball and attempts to return it even though it is very difficult to hit at times. And through his choices and his actions, even though limited by rules, he gains a relative freeness. For beyond the rules he has many alternatives and choices, and by choosing to play within the rules already set, he leaves himself free to perform well and to make choices not covered by external rules. He does not fight what is evident. He focuses his concentration on thought and body movement to accomplish specific purposes within the rules. His choices from that point on are free, and he must take the consequences if he makes an error in judgment. He is his own man. "Only the man who makes freedom real to himself meets destiny." (29, p. 53) He takes the responsibility for his choices and for his actions within the boundaries already set by the sport. He grows and suffers within the other boundaries set up by himself.

Just as freedom of choice plays a tremendous role in what the athlete is, so does the testing process of competition. Our

39

world demands that man prove himself. We emphasize achievement, success, personal accomplishment under stress, etc. But nowhere is this testing so thorough as it is in the sports world. A man may have a perfect score one day, and fail the test completely the next. The individual might be number one in the nation one year, and on the bottom the next. It is a *continuous* testing program in athletics. What a man was able to accomplish the day before means nothing in comparison to what he can accomplish here and now and *today*. Mark Spitz said, "This was very satisfying to me, because I proved to myself I could beat him. I can't forget losing, and I never will. My worst moment was at the Olympics, and my best, maybe, was tonight." (176, p. 27) Each new minute brings the chance to prove himself, and even the proof given in one minute is of no consequence for the next moment. If he is a capable performer, he must prove so continually. The athlete never goes on tenure as the professor does. He cannot count on his financial background, his reputation, or his social status to carry him through on the sports field. He must achieve through what he is; he must excel through his freedom to respond and to react as a free individual.

Whether man succeeds or fails is often determined by his desire or his *will* to bring into reality what he seeks. Nietzsche terms it "the will to power," but in the sports world one terms it "desire" or "determination." This will to succeed is evident every day. We saw it in the 100-1 shot that the Mets would win the 1969 World Series. Many saw it in Ben Hogan's return after his near-fatal accident.

Many studies are bringing to light the fact that physical achievement can be improved through mental thought. Skill reaches a higher plateau when one can mentally concentrate on the movements and the reality of accomplishment. Perhaps this is why upsets happen so often. The players *think* more about that particular game or event than the ones before or after it, and *will* success. "It is only by risking our persons from one hour to another that we live at all. And often enough our faith beforehand in an uncertified result *is the only thing that makes the result come true*." (86, p. 59)

Man survives the testing of athletics only in reference to his will to survive. In his freedom of thought, he focuses his attention on that which he would like to do and to be, and through the power of this will he steps into a relationship with reality. In a way, he says: "I will it to be so, therefore it is."

Spirit and the will to achieve and excel stay with the athlete much longer than his trophies and his broken records. Anyone who has been in the heat of competition has at one moment or another been aware that it is the striving that is important. It is the actual struggle and the actual *chancing* of defeat as well as victory that makes the difference. Theodore Roosevelt said:

> Far better it is to dare mighty things, to win glorious triumphs, even though checkered by failure, than to take rank with those poor spirits who neither enjoy much nor suffer much, because they live in the gray twilight that knows not victory nor defeat. (14, p. 847)

Courtesy of Brevard College.

One *wills* to be in the midst of the competition. One voluntarily steps forth to meet what is there, rather than walking away from it. "But when he has *found*, his heart is not turned from them, though everything now meets him in the one event." (29, p. 80) One *meets* the challenge rather than running from it. "The only thing I get satisfaction from is accomplishing something I'm not supposed to be able to do. I live for challenges, and once I overcome them I have to go on to something new," said Sam McDowell. (98, p. 36)

All athletes, at some time or another, are flat or find *nothing* in their performance. For some reason, you can't find or reach what you feel should be there, or what the situation has the potential of offering. We may *want* to feel the closeness and the being and the sense of life . . . yet nothing happens to us. There has to be something *beyond* the human will, if we *sincerely* want a "happening" and cannot bring it about. Many times, we don't find anything because what we *really* want is to win—not to find our *being* through an openness to life. Other times, we find that *something* only through a process we do not understand and know only as *chance*. By chance it is there and we are there. And we meet it because of our thereness and its presence.

If the athlete were to enter into sport without there being anything beyond what he already knows about himself, then it would turn out to be a meaningless experience. There would be a *nothing* beyond the present. Man cannot choose what part of himself he wishes to carry into sport. He carries everything about himself into the action. Sometimes, the individual understands what he carries, because he knows himself quite well. Other times, the individual is unaware of what he is, even though it is all there with him. A man can't *will* himself to be open to what is around or within himself. It is there, and whether he finds meaning or not is beyond his ability to will it. However, the sport situation is such that one rarely goes away without discovering something unknown about the self. One does not go into a situation filled with stress and conflict without coming face to face with what *is*. When standing with your back against the wall, it is very hard to lie to yourself. In a case like this, you either fight or you back off, but at any rate you *know* what kind of a person you were at that point of decision. And if it is true that man learns more about himself during the competitive situation, then a *zero* situation has not existed, and the athlete has walked away with meaning of some kind. Discovery of self is no small thing, and even when found in small degrees, a realization of being is far from nothingness, and therefore does have meaning for the individual. "Indeed, what creates in me consciousness of self is the consciousness I have of a not-self. . . . " (217, p. 125)

But regardless of the *potential* that is there . . . we must not forget that it is beyond the ability to *will* what we would wish to find. To have important relationships with teammates and with opponents, one must really want to meet on a common and humanistic ground. There is something within the person that says "hello" to the self of others. But one cannot *make* oneself do this. One can't say that today I am going to be open to this humanistic meeting through competition. In a way, we voluntarily open ourselves to this humanistic meeting and in a way we are *opened* to it. "The *Thou* meets me. But I step into direct relation with it. Hence the relation means being chosen and choosing. . . . " (29, p. 11)

Perhaps this is what is meant by "playing for the breaks," the *real* breaks. We continue to try. We tackle, we strive, we hit the shots, we slide hard, we charge the boards—all with the hope, and not the assurance, that we will achieve the meeting. Perhaps in all honesty it can be said that the sport performer does this more with hopes of game-victory than for actualization of humanity. (202, p. 69)

Chapter 2

SPORT: MEANING THROUGH WHOLENESS

The movement patterns of the athlete give a sense of excitement, of emotion. The crowds sense the electricity, the charge
being given off by the continuous movement exhibited by
physically skilled individuals. There is no status quo in athletics.
Everything that happens is in a continuously changing state.
Defensive and offensive patterns change. Movements fluidly
change into other patterns, and strategy flows from one line of
thought into another. One could not describe accurately what
goes on in a ballgame if he wanted to. What is happening goes
beyond logic and statistical description, because it is *more* than
physical movement . . . it is thought and emotion and feeling
and being all tied into one dynamic and ever-changing whole.
Man *is*, and *was*, and *becomes* in sport. What one sees and senses
while watching the athlete who is *really* involved is a *total existence* of that individual. Every iota of his being is tied up in just
that . . . *being*. He is *involved*, without any strings attached.

There is no isolated part of the athlete. According to Torben
Ulrich, "There is not necessarily more depth to me in music
than in tennis or anything. I simply try to do everything as well
as I can. Everything is a fitting part of everything else I do."
(108, p. 84) One may be able to evaluate some aspects of the
athlete—his physical attributes for instance—but this is only a
part of him. His emotions must also be evaluated, and we do
not know how to do this yet. Nor do we know how to evaluate
the spiritual, or the many mental factors.

The athlete exists through his physical being . . . but he also
exists through his personal, *intimate* being, which might be
classified as the emotional self. He goes beyond the objective,
and our ability to measure objectively. How can one describe
the intense desire to win "the big one," or the wish to throw a
perfect fifty-yard touchdown pass? How can one tell another

44

what he feels when he reaches a crisis in his performance, and everything hinges on a split-second decision, or even on chance? How does one explain what one feels as he runs and jumps, and is caught up in the action? These are things that involve the total being, and they are not subject to evaluation or description . . . but they are imperative to the athlete's *existence*. He is *in all* of his being.

There is probably no other area in our society where the totality of man is tested so severely or so often as in sport. It is impossible to participate in athletics with isolated parts of the mind or the body. When the man steps on the field, he is *all* there, and every part of him goes through the test.

> It is clear that everything which the individual experiences may be said to have a twofold nature. It is both a single thing and also a sum of parts—a unity and a plurality. (185, p. 48)

One should not think of sport as an experience that simply sweeps the athlete along. Man can pretty well control his own fate on the athletic field, provided he is willing to go beyond the state of nothingness of just existing, and become *really* involved in the action. Just to go through the movements or just to have the necessary physical coordination to stay afloat in the pool is not enough. There is much more to the movement than *just* the movement. There is a point where the physical and mental, and even spiritual qualities of the athlete meet. It is here, in the full committment and complete involvement, that man begins to sense the *wholeness* of his being. He no longer is in the water. He *swims* in the water.

The athlete lays his emotions and his mental attributes on the line as well as his physical skills. There is no armchair approach. There is no easy way. If he can't live with the pain and the conflict of emotions, then he can't live with the test, for there is no separation of the good and the bad. As Nietzshe said, "He who has a *why* to live can bear with almost any *how*." He can't pick out what he chooses as far as his being is concerned . . . it is all there to act and to be acted upon as he participates. One reason man finds wholeness when engaging in sport is that there can be no holding back of *parts* of him if he *truly* participates. He can't hide away parts of himself for another day if he *really* plays. The man who sits may have proven his mind, but he has never proven his body. On the athletic field, one proves the mind and the body. One proves *the man*, or one doesn't.

He loves the feel of strong muscles,
The cooling roll of perspiration,
The throbbing of a good heart-beat.
He likes the thrill of sound competition,
The driving will of determination,
The jarring when two bodies meet.
He takes the aches of new bruises,
The tearing hurt of torn tendons,
The ripping scrapes of solid falls.
He feels the pain of legs cramping,
The crying need of lungs winded,
The knocks while chasing the ball.

He knows the high price of effort,
The shaming prick of swollen pride,
The nagging need for playing fair.
He knows the joy of shared laughter,
The meaning of remorseful tears,
The pushing effect of a dare.
He knows the bumps of hard hustle,
The jerking stops on sore ankles,
The searching shot of unsure hand.
He knows the worth of scars endured,
The pulsing beat of true victory—
The playing heart of plucky man.*

One just cannot separate existence and meaning in the sports world, or for that matter, it is hard to separate purpose and value in athletics. Sport does not encourage separation. It forces

* "The Athlete," by Patsy Neal. Originally printed in *The Christian Athlete*, 9:14, January, 1965. Used by permission.

unification . . . or else the individual finds he is not fit to remain in competition.

The values we accept in our world are the same values we carry into the playing field. If we accept that all life is competition, as our competitive society would have us believe, then it would be hard to carry an opposing value of cooperation into the athletic event. If our striving in the world is for materialistic gains, it would be impossible to *authentically* seek spiritual levels in competition. In other words, there are not *two* worlds: the one out there and the one on the athletic field.

Experience in sports allows contact with other aspects of life. It establishes relationships in other realms. One of the most important lessons I learned about life resulted from my first competitive experience against the Russian All-Star team. The tour involved a series of games in the states, including Madison Square Garden, and was set up between Russia and the United States as an exchange program in basketball.

I'm not too sure what I was expecting to encounter when we met the Russians, but as usual I was too unprepared to be prepared. Their men's team and their women's team looked so similar to all previous humans that I had met, that I was disillusioned to find these people were Russians.

It only took a few good screens and several fast-breaks down the court before I realized that regardless of where they parked their tennis shoes, the Russian women got the job done.

While losing to this surprisingly powerful and well coordinated team, it slowly sank into my dull head that something a lot more important than a series of basketball games was going on. Even with the language barrier, we were finding a greater means of communication than mere words. We substituted smiles and sign language for ordinary well-formed sentences. We shook hands instead of rattling on endlessly about odds and ends usually encountered in introductions. We understood small signs of courtesy even while the language accompanying it made no sense.

We talked not as Americans to Russians, or Russians to

47

Americans, but more basically as people to people. And the result was amazing. They ceased to be "those Russians." They instead became individuals with backgrounds. They became men and women who worked and played as we did—who had homes and families—who ate and slept and hoped and laughed and cried. They became individuals with individual needs and individual rights.

We became more and more acquainted with their lives in their country as the days went by. We used interpreters to ask questions of each other and to discover what men feel and what individuals do when living on opposite sides of the planet.

The first few days we ate, we slept, we played ball, and we talked as best we could. But we weren't too busy playing ball and talking to the women's team to forget that there was also a men's team from Russia on the tour with us. Some of the players were aggressive on the ballcourt—but undoubtedly the trait didn't end there.

It wasn't long before comments were heard about how cute so-and-so was, or what darling eyes a certain guard had. One guy, Guram Minashvili, had all the girls ready to trade Elvis for him—and to throw Rock Hudson in to boot. He called one of the girls on the phone, but since neither of them could speak the other's language, they spent a good 15 minutes just giggling over the phone. It sounded like a pretty intelligent conversation to me.

The men and women showed signs of a new Russia—intelligence matched with physical fitness. One sensed that their country was no longer a country of backward people. During the tour, and as we traveled from city to city and played in one gym and then in another, I felt that for the first time in my life I was beginning to realize the stuff that really makes up men, regardless of the texture of their skin or the location of their birth or the culture of their society.

I caught a glimpse of the smile that comes from happiness and the hurt in the eyes that comes from sadness.

I saw a 7'3" woodcuter from Latvia eat the same type of food I was eating and knew that all men meet hunger in the same way.

48

I watched a player take a hard fall and saw the pain on her face—and I knew that hurt travels throughout the world, and every individual is subject to it.

I ran side by side with Russian players on a ball court, and their legs jumped and ran in the same way mine did—and I knew that all men sought pleasure through sports and recreation.

I asked questions by way of an interpreter and received answers—and I was sure that all men thought and responded when given the chance.

I saw signs of fear from being in a strange country with strange people, and I knew that all men sought security and yet had something brave beneath the fear that made them stand like men and act like men.

I saw a Russian man stand and give an American woman his seat—and I saw an American man open the door for a Russian girl, and I knew that courtesy is a human symbol of kindness.

I saw a winner congratulate a loser and vice versa, and I couldn't stand the greatness of the thought that sportsmanship could go beyond the boundaries of a country and beyond the limitations of different languages.

I saw strangers grow to respect and understand each other—and I knew that if men and women could meet on a common ground and see what makes each other tick, then there would be less tension and more friends.

I heard their players singing an old American song with Russian words, and our hands kept time with the music—and our hearts beat the same tune—and all the time I kept thinking that all men sing and all hearts beat. Only the words were different. And then I couldn't get that thought out of my mind, that regardless of what country you went to only the words were different.*

So from this experience of playing against the Russian team,

* "Those Russians," by Patsy Neal. Originally published in Wayland College literary magazine, and then in the *Pen* (University of Utah). Used by permission.

I discovered that sport does not isolate itself to the gym floor. It is not limited by the tartan track or the gutters of the swimming pool. The relationship taking place *in* sport carries over to other aspects of life. What happens in sport reaches out and touches *everything*. What one finds meaningful in sport can also be meaningful outside of sport.

There is only the one world, and *the sports world is very much a part of the total world*. But in many cases, *more is required of the athlete* than of the individual who does not chance the complete self. One can get by while using only the mental faculties in an academic classroom. One can be involved only emotionally with a friend, or one may only be involved physically with a person . . . but when one participates in sport and competition, *one is involved,* period. All of the person takes part. The mental processes are used. The emotional aspect becomes involved, and certainly the physical is utilized. One does not just play mentally, or emotionally, or physically. *One plays*, period. And that says it. There is a *oneness* in athletics, and because of the participation of the total person, there is the chance for integration of the person. There is the chance for *wholeness*.

> In order to exist as an individual at all, one must conceive of some thread of unity on which the various parts, aspects or experiences of one's self may be said to be strung. What this means is that one must have some unified concept of oneself as an entity. (185, p. 77).

But this oneness is dependent on authentic meaning. For the athlete to experience oneness and wholeness tomorrow because of a meaningful life, the athlete must have a meaning today. The individual cannot separate meaning in time, or it becomes *meaningless*.

Most athletes are prepared for the *now*. They are ready for *today's* competition. Each time man encounters the opponent, his thoughts are tuned for that moment. "This is the big one," he says, or more commonly, "This is it." But even so, in sport there is no real separation of time. The athlete practiced yesterday to prepare for today's game. He plays the game now, but looks forward to the future chance to replay the opponent. Everything the athlete does is geared toward *unity in time*. His living and playing are continuous, without any broken edges. The past, present, and the future are all dependent upon each other. They each have their importance, and as such they form a continuum of meaning.

However, if one *says* the experience has meaning, it does not make it so. The experience has meaning only if it *really* has meaning. Consequently, if the athlete is involved in a false meaning, or if the confrontation he is experiencing in sport is *faked*, there *is no meaning*. And a *meaningful experience tomorrow;* does not come easily if it is based on a meaningless experience today. " . . . the striving to find a meaning in one's life is the primary motivational force in man." (61, p. 154) If one does become committed to a fake participation and just goes through the motions, then finding the *real thing* is that much harder. One can pretend one is *involved*, but one cannot pretend *one is*.

One soon learns not to continually seek a meaning when there is none to be found, *provided* one can recognize what is meaningful. You cannot *make* a meaningful life when there is no meaning to start with. An authentic participation in sport is doomed when it is built on artificial values. So for sport to be meaningful to the individual, it must be meaningful in an authentic way. It must be *real* to the individual, not false because one is simply *wishing* it to be real. To be real, it is sought for what is *is*, not for what one would like for it to be. Sport can be meaningful to the individual only if it is confronted in a personal way. If one wishes to be detached and aloof from the phenomenon that *is* there, then he cannot expect to confront it face to face in an *intimate* way. The promotion of wholeness is possible only if one is willing to embrace oneself as a *true* person. Unfortunately, the attainment of *complete* totality—of completeness between the individual and his environment—comes only rarely . . . for it takes more than most are willing to give to be real.

But the chance to reach it is there, and man knows it is there, if he can but open himself to it. In sport, there exists a place where a "happening" can take place that leaves man open to self-fulfilment and realization. This completeness of man and his involvement is not limited to geographical areas or to social levels. It is a thing that binds him to the universe in which he lives.

How can the individual find a meaningful experience? Is it something that comes all at once? Can you *suddenly* create something that holds meaning when all along over the years you have been committed to a false meaning? It is very hard to go from an unauthentic experience to an authentic one, in sport or in life. One must actually *experience* meaning to have meaning. One must actually *be* authentic to be authentic.

Courtesy of Brevard College. Bill Boggs, Photographer.

In short, sport offers a place where man can find *himself* meaningful. "My celebration comes from within." (125, p. 38)

Sport affirms that he *is*, and that *he is* even amid fear and turmoil. It tells him that amid all the struggle and among all the conflict, only *he is* for certain. He is not drifting, for he himself has meaning and within this meaning he is affirmed as a part of reality . . . and within himself he possesses the wholeness he has sought so long in his outer world. "I am sure that in any pursuit, especially athletics, confidence and satisfaction must come from within. If it does not, if you must find your satisfaction from without, usually from publicity and acclaim, then you can be hurt badly by losing—even if you did your best." (187, p. 86)

Perfection in Sport

Perhaps it is this glimpse at wholeness that pushes a man to perfect his skills in sport. And although no athlete ever reaches a plateau where he can do everything right every time ["An athlete's makeup is such that it is physically and emotionally impossible to perform in every race as you are capable of performing in *certain* races" (197, p. 25)], there is a certain amount of perfection in sport. The ball goes through and doesn't touch the rim. The bowler hits a 300 game. The archer hits the bull's-eye every time during an end. However, the *overall* performance is never perfect. The bowler might have been off balance or an inch off target and *still* have gotten the strike. The basketball player might have aimed for the rim and *still* made the basket as a result of a banked shot. The archer might have been off in her sighting, but *still* hit the bull's-eye because of a sudden gust of wind.

Even while knowing it is impossible, everyone tries to reach the ideal. The athlete tries to have the "perfect" performance; he tries to reach that which no man before him has reached. In John Rinka's words, "Basketball enabled me to discover the true feelings that accompany the pursuit of perfection. I now can appreciate what a musician experiences as he strives for the perfect blending of notes, or a writer for the perfect arrangement of words, or an electrician for the precise alignment of circuits. I can also appreciate the feeling when failure occurs." (170, p. 9)

Searching for perfection, is it any wonder that so many feel they are failures? We strive for unreachable goals. We work for perfection when the ultimate is out of the human reach. But it is in the struggle where man finds himself . . . not in the attain-

-ment only. Sport is made up of struggle . . . sport *is* struggle.

Many become wrapped up in skiing because of the challenge to confront the elements with the body and to come out with the perfect run, or the complete turn. The same is true with surfing. One must master the self *and* the environment, or else the chance for completeness is gone in a moment. It is probably this freedom to fail or succeed, dependent upon one's sense of balance with the world, that attracts so many to surfing. It is man against nature—he is competing on his own—and every wave he attempts to ride is different; therefore, demanding a different reaction and the ability to adjust *then and there*. Joyce Hoffman said, "Surfing's really neat. The ocean and the mountains are the neatest. . . . Every wave is different. Every beach is different. It's really a neat feeling, this big thing between you and nature . . . you're mastering nature, you're making the wave give you something." (180, p. 110) Each confrontation is a new challenge—the athlete is riding between a world of reality and intimate failure—what happens depends completely on how he reacts to each given moment. He has the ability to make it, or he must face the fact he has been "wiped out" by his inability. The responsibility for success or failure is his and his alone. He can't blame others, for it is *he* that rides the board. The environment, the current, the wave, the wind are part of the sport, and if he takes part in it, he must accept it *all*. If he seeks the perfect ride, he must take the risk that he can control *everything* that goes along with it, and that includes his self and any fear that might arise from his daring. He is what he is . . . all alone on the board . . . determining his own action, and as a result, the consequences. He finds his perfection in his *being*. For a moment, or maybe even for a minute or two, *he controls* his world *if* he has the ability and the guts . . . and this is what it is all about. He is *if* he is. What he finds out during the ride is the reality of himself in that point in time . . . and he can't fake it. He is capable *or* he isn't.

In sport, one has the *chance* to transcend imperfection and to reach the ultimate, even if for just a second. And if one doesn't make it, he has the freedom to choose and to dare *again*. It never ends with one wave if one has courage. Without the courage, there is no *chance* for anything. The taking part with the *whole* self is the perfection. The movement on the board doesn't have to be a thing of beauty as long as the *feel* is there. The surfer communicates with the power under his board. He controls it as a part of his action, even though the wave has the power to "wipe" him out forever. There is a relationship between the daring and the power. One flows into the other, and as a result one *exists* in the truth of the forces around, about, and *within*. One perfects one's potential beyond the boundaries of fear. One finds *value* in being alive . . . and in *seeking* perfection.

Creativeness of Athletes

Man, in his search for wholeness, often creates new things. He finds that in expressing himself, he brings about things that have a different form because they reflect his own uniqueness. He is different; therefore, his products are different. Many times, the creativeness on the part of the individual is a result of his attempt to get away from the conventional . . . to change the status quo.

However, most athletes stay with the conventional, because their interest lies in achieving results, and the conventional way of performing has *proven* itself as a means of achieving a certain level of accomplishment. But every once in a while, a few rare individual athletes do strike out on their own and seek expression in new, untried ways. They in a sense, create new techniques. At times, this happens by accident. At other times, it grows out of unique individual desire for a *personal* type of expression. At other times, rational thought produces new means of achieving good performance. The "Forsburg Flop" was a very personal thing, and certainly would not work for everyone—but other athletes' styles and techniques have been copied with great success by thousands.

Creativeness on the part of the athlete comes in many ways . . . sometimes in such small degrees that others are unaware of it . . . but it is a result of the individual looking for a newness of life, for the point of exhilaration. Creativeness reconfirms a person's uniqueness. It tells him that he is *there* . . . that he is contributing just as the artist, musician, writer, and painter is. "I look upon basketball as a form of synchron- ized movement," said John Rinka. "It is the fluidity of five people intertwining towards a single goal. It is a form of individual expression, too, and must be viewed as a performing art. The court, itself, is really a stage." (170, p. 9)

In performing, the athlete starts in "nothingness." There are the inanimate objects to be used, the floor or field space, the oxygen in the air, and *himself*. It is the athlete's *action* that creates something in this boundary of nothingness, for without him the space, the oxygen, and the inanimate objects are not *used*. It is *his* movement that creates. It is his performance that brings a *realness* to a nothingness. His being is *reality*, and what he does in those moments of competition *is everything*. "The performer, as he moves, transforms non-being into being in the world of nothingness." (202, p. 110)

Sport does not offer an empty space away *from* the world. It offers the tools to carry something relative and relevant *into* the world. Man may not understand all that is happening around him or that is present in his environment, but he must *attempt* to understand if he is to live with himself easily.

Sport is not *all* of life . . . but it is a vital part. According to Don Schollander, "The person who is *just* an athlete or *just* a student has a very hollow life [italics mine]." (181, p. 26) If one is incapable of *living* on the basketball court, it is unlikely one is capable of living well off it. There is so much to be created out of the nothingness that exists around us—and the boundaries are so unlimited in the sports world to be creative since so much of the individual is tied up in the "happening."

Basically, however, sport is pretty much structured; patterns of play are pretty much systematized, and the limits and boundaries of man's actions are pretty much rational. Yet, it is recognized that even among the structure and rationality, there is the fact that achievements go beyond the rational . . . that performance sometimes becomes great or magnificent because of unknown factors . . . that emotions and undefined human qualities sometimes lift the athlete above any rational calculation of his ability. *Something* in man creates his *own* greatness.

Chapter 3

THE RATIONAL AND PRAGMATIC IN SPORT

We should never make the mistake of trying to understand man purely on a rational level. He has many more sides, and he does idiotic things at times. A common expression in athletics is "How could I be so stupid?"

There is always the attempt at perfection, often done through rational thought, scheduling, and training methods. But beyond the rational routine, there is a function that has no rational structure.

> To propose that man is in sport because he should be, or that he participates as a result of knowledge of and commitment to a value, vastly oversimplifies the situation. Man is in sport or dance on grounds independent of the practical or rational. (110, p. 58)

Call it a mystical dimension, or a religious experience, or anything you like. But it's *there*. One *explores* the self and the world and his surroundings in a way that cannot be explained or rationalized. One is *aware* of things that one cannot explain. One *understands* things that he cannot describe . . . about himself, about the world. One participates without knowing *why* at times. One plays because one *must*, whether one has the answers or not.

Paradoxically, man becomes more human as he seeks to go beyond his rational thought which has set him apart from other living things. He goes *beyond* that which he knows and which he can explain in rational terms, and as a result he *humanizes* himself. His achievement is not in accumulating facts . . . but in *doing*.

It might be termed irrational to submit the body to such

exhaustion, pain, and extensive training as the athlete does. But if the only other alternative to the athlete is to be "half-alive," as a result of a more sedative life, then even though this torture in itself might seem to be ridiculous, the alternative gives it a meaning of rationality.

It seems even more ridiculous to keep reminding ourselves "it is only a game" when the being is so completely submerged in the action. It is *real,* and as such is not "just a game."

When the athlete is faced with the choice between the hard and the easy, between exhaustion and rest, between any two alternatives that have *meaning* to him or *lack of meaning* to him as an athlete, he throws open a door to his search for *real* answers. He balances values; he pits one desire against another; he weights the cost. And when the decision is made, he either becomes richer or poorer—according to his awareness of what he is and what he wants to be—and how much he is willing to pay to become or to be. "My blood was fired with a new enthusiasm. I relished the exhausting workouts—the harder the better. I was not alone. I was one of many young men reaching for the sky. The outdoor elements, rain or snow, did not deter us. There was a job to be done and we were about to do it well." (49, p. 21)

And even though this thing called "sport" he may be so immersed in, may not seem to be logical or to fit the mould of reason at times, it is a necessary part of his desire to *live* . . . making it a rational thing to do. Yet, even though in a world of order, the rules of sport may seem sensible, the contradictions ever present between the "letter of the law" and the "spirit of the rules," continuously remind the athlete that in many ways sport is *absurd.*

So one must realize that sport is full of contradictions. It is heroic to beat a man to his knees inside the ring, but not outside it. It is justifiable to "foul" to get the ball in the closing seconds of a ballgame, but not sportsmanlike to foul in such a manner that injury results. It is all right to bean a batter from the other team if *their* pitcher beans one of your batters first. It is even possible for a man to be a whiz in figuring out the defensive patterns of the opponent in football, but a dud in the classroom.

Courtesy of Brevard College.

There are other contradictions. The athlete logically goes about trying to perfect certain movements, even though he *knows* perfection is not possible. The bowler can*not* bowl a 300 game every day. The basketball player can*not* hit 100% every game. Yet, the continuous practice goes on, and perfection that cannot be perfected is sought. If the athlete *really* thought he could reach perfection, then the continuous seeking would be ridiculous. But the perfection one seeks is relative; therefore, absurdity becomes more logical. One seeks to do *his* best rather than to be perfect. One seeks to break the record rather than run the *perfect* race. One tries to reach *his potential* rather than attempting to go beyond what is there. " ... some people always expect you to be the best, which isn't quite the same thing as *doing* your best. Nobody, and I don't give a damn who he is, or what sport we're talking about, can be at his peak all the time." (197, p. 25)

The athlete is concerned with perfection, but knowing he can never reach perfection, he pursues that which he thinks he can obtain in the hope that it will lead him to something more. The athlete seeks *everything* by attempting that which he thinks is possible. Absurd? Maybe. Meaningful? Yes.

Sport sometimes seems absurd because we can't explain everything that happens to us while participating. Why is it that we never know beforehand how well we are going to perform? You would think that after years of practice, one could reasonably predict what type of performance one will turn in on a certain night, but all athletes know this is not possible. Terry Bradshaw, a quarterback who many feel is destined for greatness in pro football, had this to say after a bad game: " . . . I felt so good, so loose. And then I did so poorly. I couldn't figure it out." (243, p. 60)

We should never limit our thoughts to only reasonable answers when dealing with sport and competition. In the 1940s, it was *unreasonable* to assume a man could run a four-minute mile. Today, it is unreasonable to assume he can't. Rational thought by most fans and sport writers would never have placed the Jets over the Baltimore Colts in the 1969 Super Bowl (or the Chiefs over the Vikings in he 1970 Super Bowl). Yet, one man felt it was unreasonable to pick the game any other way. Joe Namath "guaranteed" a victory for the Jets over the Colts and proceeded to prove the reasonableness of his belief.

Man is restricted by nature and natural forces around him as he competes. Gravity creates certain limits, just as oxygen supply in high altitudes sets its own boundaries for endurance performance. Sport does not free man *from* his nature, but rather binds him to create and to develop *within* his natural limitations.

Even though limited by his natural environment, he does have *freedom of choices*. In fact, he is almost forced into choosing because of the many alternatives he is faced with in his effort to learn to control his performance. It becomes frustrating because what the athlete hopes to achieve may not be attainable for him at that moment and point in time. He may become aware that what he seeks is too much, and as tension and feelings of near failure build up within him, he may choose another alternative as an objective that might be more easily achieved—he might relinquish the dream of a perfect performance for a win regardless of how close the final score might be—or he might give up the hopes for victory in one brief moment that might involve a "personal happening."

Man is human, and doesn't always act rationally. He tries to fling himself higher through the forces of gravity. He tries to run faster against the wind and the forces thrown up by nature to resist his movement. He tries to exert mental powers over inanimate objects as he trains to put the ball through a small space, and to propel a tiny golf ball into the hole many hundreds of yards away. He tries to control his movements to such an extent that he can exert his being over the environment around him even though he *knows* all the discipline in the world will not take him beyond the limits exerted *on* him by nature.

So he fights with the absurdity of trying to live with the tension created by his own decision to go beyond what other men have done . . . to break records, to be *the* best. He creates his own world of anxiety as he wonders if his pain and anguish in the past months of training have been sufficient to carry him to *that* moment of glory . . . ["When the swimmers took their marks, Spitz felt so tight—and was quivering so much—he jumped into the water for a false start. . . . " (176, p. 27)]. He wonders if the endless hours of practice will carry him to that point in time when he has done the *impossible*, when he has accomplished what he had only *hoped* to do. Rod Laver once said, "I've lived for tennis, and to hear yourself called the best ever at what you've lived for—well, it made me turn over a little inside." (213, p. 70)

But if his dreams carry him too far, and if the tension in his being becomes too great, and he no longer can *hope* for the accomplishment of that which he strives for, then he either quits or he faces reality and changes his goals. He no longer seeks what he wishes to *be* and which is of real meaning to him as an athlete, but he seeks what is *obtainable*. It is at this point that the individual drops out from the meaningful life as a *being,* and tunes in to the values of the society in which he lives. He seeks that which he *can* win because it is within his realm of possiblity, and turns his back on that which offers a moment of supreme exaltation if he *chances* it . . . and *makes* it.

The rational does not guarantee meaningful experiences. Man is *more* than a being of reason. He is feeling, and sensing, and perceptions. Pete Maravich recalls a Junior Varsity game he played in with only eighty-seven people present. "I just wanted to do everything and be everything in front of that crowd. I wanted to put on such a show. I don't even remember what happened in the game; I just remember the feeling." (253, p. 40) When one "aces" the opponent, there is more than the logical thought that the opponent did not touch the serve. There is a feeling of satisfaction, of pride, and even a thrill involved in a physical act that can be *reasonably* explained. But how do you explain what you *feel* at that moment?

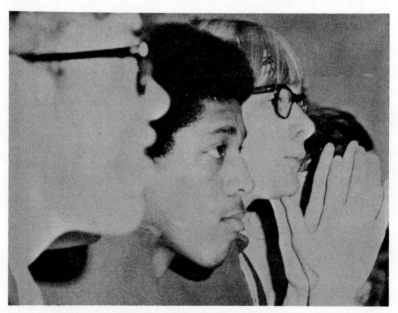

Courtesy of Brevard College. Bill Boggs, Photographer.

It is the effective realm that truly characterizes sport, and movement is *real*, not symbolic; the body is a source of sensation, and in human experience it is sensation which has the least cultural content. (59, p. 44)

To compete as a free individual, the athlete must accept the fact that sport is a situation of contradictions and absurdity. Through his free will he sets his own value system. He changes the concept of absurdity because a thing *has meaning to him*— and therefore, is no longer absurd.

To have meaning, we have to go beyond the theoretical and the pragmatic in sport. We must someway enter into the human dimension, where relationships are formed . . . with teammates, opponents, and with self. This is a place where the *being* is involved, not theoretically, not pragmatically, but in *reality*. "For I speak of nothing else but the real man, of you and of me, of our life and of our world—not of an I, or a state of being, in itself alone. The real boundary for the actual man cuts right across the world of ideas as well." (29, p. 13)

There is a fine line that is hard to describe in sport. This line separates the performance itself from the *symbolic meaning* it represents. What we actually *do* may hold meanings of great importance to us that we are not consciously aware of.

We have so many traditions in sport—the throwing out of the baseball before the World Series, the flipping of the coin before the football game, the awarding of gold medals to the winners and bronze to third place, the shaking of hands before and after the contest . . . the list is endless. What do they *mean*? Are they really connected to sport as such? What does the tradition mean to the individual and is tradition *vital* to the meaning of sport? What added dimension comes from these various functions that is not included in the *actual* performance? Does one become more aware of his human existence in sport . . . and in the *meanings* it brings as a result of these *symbolic* acts?

The retention of many traditions in sport does not seem logical today, but we must remember that man is not completely rational . . . so logic may have no place in the answers to these questions. Rather than logic, we need to understand meaning. In order to theorize, we must go to the basic individual experience, the searching for existence . . . the need to *be* . . . to be an *expressive being*. We may be aware of reality in the pragmatic function, but there is a different type of reality in what sport *represents* to the man. The symbolic is as important in reality to being, as the pragmatic.

When one speaks in terms of relationships and meaning, one must accept the fact that the individual athlete is capable of

63

thought. To be effective, athletes must think. They must transform what they experience into meaningful action. The player must analyze whether to cut right or left, pass or shoot, etc. In a sense, he must continually use the thought process to "survive" the opponent's attempt to *beat* him. The athlete must continually make split-second decisions, judge the space and environment around him in relation to himself and the opponent, and must be able to perceive what is relevant and what is not. The athlete must take what is *there*, translate it, and make something meaningful out of it. The imagination and the cognitive are important aspects of transforming the symbolic into meaningful forms and physical patterns of action through the thought process. Jim Ryun said, "I'll keep going back in my mind to the little things, positive things. I will select certain races and play them back inside my head." (157, p. 17)

The athlete fulfils many animal needs just as non-athletes do. But the athlete steps beyond animal instincts. He must actually learn to limit his biological and animal needs in order to perform as well as possible. He does this through his ability to symbolize. His innermost thoughts become expressed through the overt activity going on during play.

Man's thought process is just as important to his life as eating and sleeping, and although it is not commonly listed as such, possibly one of the most important needs a man has is to find *meaning* to his life. "There is nothing in the world . . . that would so effectively help one to survive even the worst conditions, as the knowledge that there is a meaning in one's life." (61, p. 164) This *need for meaning* gives as much craving to a man's life as any of his biological needs—and it is only through an understanding that the continuous stream of thought patterns and symbolic processes going on in a man's mind is basic to survival and to happiness that we can understand the role of sport.

Theoretically, we can form conclusions about what is actually going on within sport, forming a philosophy to guide us. Yet, these things cannot be proved . . . but neither can philosophy in other realms. This is a unique trait of man, the ability to theorize and form concepts, and consequently, to structure his own existence through this thought process.

What one theorizes, and what one actually does, is not necessarily the same in sport. One might theorize that fair play is the result of competition, and yet this individual might be the first to cheat on the number of strokes in golf. As a result of this inability to correlate the theoretical and the practical, many onlookers think of sport in terms of *only* the pragmatic, rather than in terms of the philosophical or theoretical. One must be very practical to engage in sport successfully. We come face to face with what is, or with *reality* in the sport world. One *actually* gets knocked down on the football field. One must *actually* put the ball through the hoop to score. One cannot theorize in the areas that are crucial to the participation, but one must *do* it. Yet, one must be aware of the intangibles that are not seen. We can *feel* these things; therefore, they do exist. But we cannot label them, or score points with them, or even draw comfort from them in all cases.

The focus on self and the knowing of self becomes easier when there is some logic or order to the environment around man. Sport offers this type of environment—being limited and defined by specific rules. Yet, it leaves room for the man to expand through free will and choice, and even emotion, since the "spirit of the rules" is not easily defined but yields to the individual's "feelings" of what is going on around him.

Sport, in many ways, is a reflection of our culture. But even so, it transcends existing codes and values . . . and knowledge. How can we explain everything that occurs in sport? How do we explain upsets, and "great nights," and panic by pros? Or the intense thrill from a great moment in sport?

Is it not possible that everything does not have to have an explanation, but just *is*—and is it not even possible that some things do not grow out of anything *knowable* to us? Perhaps they do not come from *anything* connected with our way of life as we *know* it rationally. Bill Bridges said, "I don't exactly remember when it was, but suddenly it spread over us. It was something that I had never experienced before, and I can't describe it. But suddenly this feeling was just with us all. . . . " (44, p. 27)

To get outside of ourselves, to experience everything that comes to us without having to label it, or even to understand it ... to accept the fact that there might be things *beyond* us that influence our lives whether we acknowledge it or not by name ... could be one of the most moving parts of our lives as human beings.

Time, Measurement, and Chance

Sport is a game of inches and seconds. A man can work all year, and lose everything by a fraction, or a woman can practice for months and lose everything in a moment. Can you imagine what it would feel like to work for four years preparing for the Olympics, and losing out in the trials by one-tenth of a second?

Some of the greatness in sport has been neglected by our use of measurements and statistics in an effort to describe tangibly what has been achieved by *untangible* resources possessed by the athlete. For instance, the gracefulness of the body's movement is delegated "points" in diving and gymnastics—as though another person's subjective judgement could adequately describe what another person has done in a creative, unique, and very personal way. Why we feel we must judge in this way in sport, and not at a ballet or an art exhibit, goes back to our concept of sport ... someone has to *win*.

Because so much emphasis is placed on tangible aspects, the athlete continually seeks to "better the record," or to do what no other before him has done. This attempt to get the physical, mental, and emotional techniques down to a fine point often leads to a mechanical-type performance. One must point her toes in a certain way while entering the water ... one must make her muscles achieve specific results consistently ... one must perform movements someone else has given a degree of difficulty to, regardless of how easy or difficult they might be to *you* as an individual. One must excel over and above what others have accomplished *physically*, even though *other* resources make the accomplishment possible. The athlete learns to think in terms of so many feet to get over the bar, or so many seconds to reach the tape. Fun and pleasure has *nothing* to do with statistics; therefore, man loses much of his emotional *joy* in the activity as he trains to achieve. "I resigned myself stoically to the task at hand. There was no escape now. My concentration was intense and I was determined to run to the best of my ability." (49, p. 22)

In many ways, this intense physical perfection is a thing to be admired—but if a man loses all sense of perspective and all feelings of enjoyment at the thing he is doing, he loses some of his dignity as a *human*. He becomes less human in order to block out distracting noises. He becomes less *feeling* because it aids his concentration. He becomes less authentic because he allows himself to be pulled by external goals and values rather than by his own inner sources. He becomes less of a *man*, and more of a machine.

It boils down to whether one is aware of the essence of his being. It is the *quality* of being able to feel and to think and to be emotionally and mentally involved, as well as physically, that makes the dividing line between the human and the animal. What a man *completely is*, is not being judged by our stop watches and our rulers . . . it is only the physical essence . . . and it is this *animal-like* ability to move gracefully, skillfully, and speedily that we compare with others . . . not the quality of emotion, or the quality of feeling, or the total quality of *being*. Pete Maravich's father touched on this aspect when he spoke of his son's poor showing in Madison Square Garden as being a "loss of animal instinct." (173, p. 22)

When one's physical essence in competition does not come up to the expectations (score-wise or time-wise), then the performance is classified as "poor." Yet, *what* goes on during the competition is a process that cannot be measured. Phil Woolpert talked about this:

> Our emphasis is so much on production, on a kind of visible *improvement*. People say to a guy, "Hey, John, you're not working up to capacity. You could be making another $100 a day. What's the matter with you, John?" But what if John wants to improve in something intangible? Human communications, maybe, or loving his neighbor or studying sunsets? By our simplistic measures of success, a man like John doesn't count. (95, p. 70)

Our society classifies non-physical actions in sport as being of no consequence because it cannot be run through a computer and filed for future references in comparing *records*. Our culture places the emphasis on *how* the event ends, or win-lost seasons. This can be measured. We can say John beat Bill 6-4, 6-2, and it is a tangible thing we can talk about and describe. It is hard to say that John didn't have his heart in it because he felt guilty about beating Bill because of psychological problems growing out of his childhood . . . or that Bill had no "feel" for the competition at that day and time because the "happening" just wasn't there. But we don't really *know* these things . . . and even if we did, we could not describe them adequately. Therefore, we seek only to better others in time and score, hardly ever to better ourselves in the quality of our *intimate* actions and reactions. Seldom do we seek the *inner* results; we almost always demand the *physical* achievements. "Perhaps it is time that man runs a mile for reasons of *relation* and not one of competition. But then this would *not be sport*. (202, p. 175)

Time sequence in sport is another thing that the athlete is concerned with, and which has a *total* relationship to the performance. J. C. Martin said, "They learned a great deal from last year, when they always seemed to be looking ahead to some series a couple of weeks off and not worrying about the importance of the game that day. You could see it clearly when you played them." (31, p. 28) Athletes never truly get away from past performances or practice. Everything one does is built on something he has done (or not done) before. Experience in the past, or lack of it, aids or hampers the athlete in the present. At the same time, the present performance will in some way affect future performances. Because of this effect of *wholeness of time*, one can never really get away from his past, or prevent the present from affecting the future. What one does *here and now* has far-reaching importance. It is important this moment, and it is important in the future. As Nietzsche described it: "Our destiny exercises its influence over us even when, as yet, we have not learned its nature: it is our future that lays down the law of our today." (14, p. 804)

This does not mean that one cannot change. It does mean that if one wishes to be different, it *takes time* to make the desired changes. If the tennis player has hit the overhead incor-

68

rectly for years, it is not likely that she can start hitting it correctly instantaneously from the moment of *wishing* to make the correction. The correct movements are developed over a period of time through thought, practice, and reform of habits built up from *past* actions. And although the correction might not result immediately, or at *that* point in time it has possibilities for perfection in the *future*.

The Intangible

So we know that sport is measured, and timed, and judged, and is influenced by time sequence. But just how much do we actually measure by objective means? There are so many things in sport that are outside the realm of rationalization and objective measurement. "The Mets have infused baseball with a special magic that transcends batting averages or errors or the length of time it takes to sit through a ball game." (12, p. 104) Elusive qualities pop up everywhere that evade reason, and this raises so many questions that may not have an answer, or that may not have an answer that we can pin down because of our ignorance of the human being. Why did Vince Lombardi get more out of his team? Why does sport make some, and break others? Why is it that when the individual feels the best, he sometimes has his worst performance, or vice versa? Why do some players play better under pressure than others? Joe Kapp doesn't give the answer to this last question, but he does explain how he feels about pressure:

Doing things the hard way is almost a life pattern with me—and I'm not complaining, I'm not whining, I revel in it. I like the heat, I like the pressure, I like being on the spot. The last thing I want to be is Mr. Cool out there. I want to get charged up, to hear the crowd, to overcome obstacles. I like being an emergency guy, an innovator, a "deviant." (100, p. 25)

One cannot measure man and describe him by facts, yet one tries to make rational decisions in sport although sport is not limited to the objective and the rational. Coaches try to evaluate their players through films, statistics, and their grading processes, but even so there is no cut-and-dried means of saying what a player *is* or can *do*. This is probably why John Rinka made this statement: "Basketball is people and it is emotion and it is release, but one cannot lose sight of it as merely something secondary in an academic climate. Statistics are one-dimensional and so is publicity. I never read about myself because only one small segment of my total person is being revealed." (170, p. 9)

Perhaps this inability to accurately describe what a man *is* by statistics is why so many general statements are used to praise particular players, such as: "He has the heart," "He is a scrapper," "He always comes through under pressure," "He gives 100 percent of his talent," etc.

Certainly we can judge how far the athlete threw the discus, or how fast the woman ran the hundred-yard dash. But don't we have to admit there was more to the athlete's performance than distance and time? What about his or her attitude? What about her determination? What about his fears and his hopes? What about the real goals sought by the athlete? What about his or her emotions as they went through the physical movements?

These are things that can probably never be measured scientifically, yet they definitely affect the athlete's performance, along with her physical and biological actions. Possibly these things such as mood, emotions, bodily sensations, mental concentration, and even philosophy of the athlete should be outside the realm of scientific analysis . . . yet, one should never doubt the power of the internal component taking part in competitive events.

However, in working out a philosophy of sport, these things must be considered even though they cannot be measured objectively. They still *exist,* and as such must be reflected within a philosophy of sport. When an athlete enters into competition, he doesn't know everything that is going to happen to him or to her. Sport is just not cognitive because of the many human elements involved. The athlete hates and loves, desires and wants, feels, and cares, and becomes *emotionally* involved. Vince Lombardi said:

A lot of what I say sounds corny out of context, I

70

know. It's better in the heat of the moment. But it is *me*. Hell, I'm an emotional man. I cry. I cried when we won the Super Bowl and I cried when I left Green Bay, now. I'm not ashamed of crying. Football's an emotional game. You can't be a cold fish and go out and coach. If you're going to be involved in it, you gotta take your emotions with you, mister. (93, p. 30)

Courtesy of Brevard College. Kenton Deardorff, Photographer.

These emotions are things that cannot be measured, but are there. Any philosophy concerning sport, therefore, has to consider the human element. Awareness that the human carries purposeful action and unique attributes into the action must be of utmost importance in forming a philosophy of sport.

One thing about sport and the tensions involved while playing, is that it gives the athlete the chance to adjust in a relatively *short* period of time. The game itself is cut off from everyday life; therefore, one is tired for only minutes and hours—rather than for years. One is in pain only temporarily, rather than for eternity due to lack of oxygen. One experiences extreme

71

emotions such as anger and frustration during the quarters and halves of the game, but the intenseness usually disappears at the end of the competition (although it may return the next time the same opponent is played).

Fortunately, one cannot continue *endlessly* to shoot goals or to surf or to dash one hundred yards. There is always a cut-off point in sport where one can recuperate before the *next* involvement. Possibly because of this, the *everyday* world man lives in is thought of as being cut off from the sport world. The sport world and *the* world are not cut off from each other, even though one enters into sport knowing that it is not an endless process, but that it has time dimensions just as well as rule dimensions. What happens on the sport field stands on its own, and one need not carry the agony and the esctasy into *real* life. But if the athlete really finds his authentic existence on the sport field, then he finds that sport is not a segmented part of life, but that it is a very vital part of *everything* he does in life. The great dancer, Rudolf Nureyev, evidently understood this when he said: "Life really revolves around performance. Everything offstage should be channeled for that short experience . . . but what you remember is the great privilege, the sense of accomplishment, and that time goes very fast and you must not waste a second." (189, p. 117)

So one mingles into the other. If the individual is a *real* person on the athletic field, then he is *real* off it. If he fakes his experiences on the soccer field, then he is a fake away from it. One cannot be real one minute and false the next. When one exists in reality as one is . . . then one exists in reality as one is.

A life with meaning cannot be built on artificial objectives, but the individual's goals and desires must be authentic. The person must be involved; he or she must be tied up in the present moment as well as the future possibilities. Only *personal* commitment can be meaningful. It is this necessity to become *involved*, the need to be *committed*, that gives the athlete the chance for wholeness or completeness. There is no other way. The individual cannot hold back or cling to parts of the self and try to save for another day or another time . . . the chance for living is *now*. When the athlete loses his involvement, he loses the need to participate, as well as the meaning that comes from the participation. "There are professionals and there are mercenaries in sports. The difference between them is that the professional is involved. I was never a mercenary. If I continued to play, I'd become a mercenary because I'm not involved anymore." (186, p. 18)

Even though the sport situation continually changes, man seeks some type of consistency . . . of permanence that does not alter with the direction of the play. Some things he can predict: the height of the goal from the floor, the dimensions of the playing field; but these things hold no real meaning to him as an individual. They are "things," and as such are relatively unimportant to a being who is seeking *more* than existence. In some ways, he can predict what others will do. He knows that the offensive player will shoot for the goal when open and in scoring territory. He knows that the opponent will swing at balls in the strike zone in most cases. But even here there is not real stability. The basketball player may wait until he is in a spot he feels he can hit from more effectively. The variables are constantly shifting, and as such have no real permanence. When one recognizes what *is*, one becomes secure in the knowledge because the security comes only from *within*. It is the *being* that is constant, but again there is a paradox. Consciously, one may not *know* the self. Subconsciously, one may not recognize the *real* being. So only and *if* one knows the self is there real permanence. When one really meets himself as a *friend*, then one has begun to arrive. It is impossible to determine whether this *knowing of the self* comes as a result *of* the sport situation, or is *in* the sport, but the important thing is that it *does* exist. One can discover himself while participating in sport. One can touch on security by saying "hello" to the being while competing. One can control oneself even while not being able to control external factors. Joe Kapp says: " . . . if you're doing your best, then winning isn't so crucial. A football isn't round, and you don't always have control of whether you win or lose, but you do have control of your own effort and your own mind." (99, p. 27) As a result of this control, one becomes personal with what *is* within the body, and *of* the body. So sport does offer the chance for finding the self or "realness," but at no time *guarantees* one will find it. Some do, and some don't. Why and why not?

One of the interesting facets of sport is the fact that a certain percentage of the variables cannot be predicted. One can anticipate certain moves of the opponent, but is "outguessed" on others. One can predict which way a basketball will bounce, but not a football. One can choose one team over another with a certain point spread, but there is always the unpredictable upset. Even though one knows what shots should be used during a tennis match, there are several alternatives, and it is impossible to predict which alternative or what surprise tactic the opponent will use. He should hit down the line on a specific return shot . . . but what about the lob or the crosscourt shot, or even the shot hit right at the individual? What if he misjudges his swing, and though he intended for the ball to go to a specific spot, it bounces off the wood in the opposite direction for a point? This is the exciting thing about sport. There are so many *ifs*. *If* I do this, he *should* respond in a certain way, but what *if* he doesn't? If I move here, he should move there, but he *could* go another way. I could hit his fast ball, but what *if* he throws the curve?

Considering the fact that our world is practically run by computers that can give the answer in a matter of seconds, it is refreshing to take part in an activity such as sport where rationality and predictability are not the sole controlling factors. One has a *chance* in sports. "If the ball bounces right," any team can upset any other team on a certain day. "If we are lucky," we can beat this team tonight. "One break," and we can knock this ballgame wide open. These are common phrases used by coaches and players, and exemplifies the fact that sport is a game of chance in many instances. Many players, and many coaches will admit that they won a particular contest purely by "luck." Willie Shoemaker attributes much of his success to luck: " . . . I am proud of my profession as a jockey and I am the first to realize that without lots of luck and assistance along the way it would have been impossible." (197, p. 21)

And where there is luck or chance operating, there is hope. One "hopes" for victory. One "takes a chance" that a certain strategy will confuse the opponent long enough to have its effects on the outcome of the game. One looks for the *good* bounce in a crucial situation. One hopes that it is his "lucky" day.

In all sports, there is this element of "chance." The softball player in many instances simply tries to make contact with the ball and hopes it will ricochet off in a direction that will result in a hit. The tennis player might hit the ball with the intention of passing the net player for a point, only to have a mishit send the ball over the opponent's head for an "unearned" point (why do athletes say "sorry" when ball hits net and goes over, or when unexpected and uncontrollable things happen?).

This thing called "chance" is also operating when the basketball player attempts to pull down an offensive rebound but instead tips the ball in for two points by "accident." The bowler might hit off the pocket, and yet get a strike because of the unpredictable falling of the pins. The speedball player might score a goal because of a deflection off the goal post rather than unskilled play by the goalie. Sport in many cases is a game of *chance* . . . and as such, gives hope to millions. It just might be *my* day. This is my *chance* to be a hero. He made a "once in a million shot," and became a celebrity overnight.

We just cannot completely control objects and individuals in sport. The unexpected continually happens (football players have come off the bench to tackle opponents on the way to the goal line). Coaches play the percentages, but they do not always work—and the fact that one feels one must base play on a percentage outcome reinforces the fact that many things in sports just "happen."

The Mets have made the impossible seem possible by their play in the 1969 World Series. As an article in *Newsweek* described it: "The Orioles weren't up against a team; they were up against a group of magical kids who were living out a beautiful, impossible dream." (11, p. 108) As the saying goes, "They came and conquered." But what happened between the lean years and the fat year were things that no one could have predicted or expected. Even their winning of the World Series was unexpected (as was their showing the following year since they did not repeat the right to play in the World Series). This realm of unpredictability in sport is possibly one of the many factors that makes athletics so appealing to the public and to the performer.

Every individual has his own reason for enjoying sports . . . from the "chance" offered for victory, to the financial gain, to the awareness of a *personal* relationship to life. But regardless of why he participates, and how he is bound by dimensions of time, space and the unpredictable, the athlete comes into contact with *all* of sport, not just the one purpose he began with. He may start to achieve one specific objective, but once involved, he is faced with the other meanings present. Some remain closed to these experiences because they aren't willing to accept a different type of feeling that might change their everyday *existence*. Some don't want to veer from the immediate goal to seek other aspects and values. Some just refuse to admit there is more there.

Because the situations in sport are continually changing, it requires adjustment on the part of the individual since the problems faced by athletes are never fully solved. The tennis player may learn how to cope with the slice serve, but then when the opponent senses this and goes to the twist, another door must be opened. There is always a defense to figure out, or a reaction to counteract another reaction, and the new problems must be dealt with as they crop up. Perhaps, the fact that man's solution to stress situations in sport is never the same because the problems vary so, is what makes many shy away from the involvement.

Those who dare to be involved find out early that there is no single answer, and the player must solve what he can at *that* moment, and during *that* game, and then he must be courageous enough to come back to solve *more* problems the next day . . . and the next.

The joy of sport is a thing of *now*. It is this moment, and this time, and this space that counts. And when the being is thrilled with its own existence at that moment, the whole body hopes that the next second and the next minute and the next hour will be just like that. Sport gives ecstasy by *saying* something meaningful to the individual. "I guess I love the game of basketball more than anything else in the world," said Pete Maravich.

"From the beginning it was like an addiction with me." (253, p. 39) The athlete senses an animal vitality . . . even more marvelous because it is combined with the human element of *feeling and thinking*. He finds pleasure and joy in his physical movement, and satisfaction in his awareness. A great runner, Kipchoge Keino, explains it this way: "If I give everything in me, how can I be unhappy? You have to lose sometimes. You may be top today. But tomorrow it's not going to be as today." (140, p. 25)

Chapter 4

HAVING A TRUENESS IN SPORT

There are many superficial things going on in the sport world: the rituals before the games, the eye-catching and expensive uniforms, the emphasis on pageantry and patriotism such as the playing of the national anthems and the placement of athletes on platforms at the Olympics, etc. The public enjoys the splendor of these rituals, and even though they may not add much to the actual performance that takes place on the playing field, they add to the overall program as far as spectators are concerned.

The public places great emphasis on many extrinsic values, and when athletes gear their performance toward pleasing the public in order to have larger gate returns, many of the internal values of a quieter nature go unnoticed. As a result, many athletes never go beyond the superficial awards connected with their sport. A few, however, seek more. And in their search they open themselves to intrinsic values which lead from emptiness to being. They look beyond the superficial values imposed by cultural standards, and seek realness in their *own* lives.

But almost every athlete has "false" moments. They tend to fake many things, especially the movements of more successful athletes. Many took up the Forsberg "flop." Many have copied the style of Cousey and Billie Jean King, even though the specific movements may not be natural or efficient for them as individuals. We see this mimicry in so many ways. The volleyball player mimics other well-known volleyball players as she serves the ball. The little league football player patterns his movements after the well-known professional although he does not understand nor feel a part of the movement. The swimmer copies the "perfect" stroke and uses it although she doesn't become a real part of the stroke, but just goes through the motions. All of these examples are indicative of falseness.

In these cases, the performer is not *really* a part of what he or she is doing. The individuals are going through the motions in a certain point in time and space, but the motions are isolated from the self. He or she is not *completely* involved in hitting the serve, or doing the flutter kick. There is no authentic tie between the movement and the person—it is a copy and not a unified thing. There is no *real* giving of self to the hit or the stroke . . . it is just done.

Perhaps this explains in a way the difference between performances during practice and the *real* performance during a match or a game. There always seems to be that "something extra" during the actual competition. Even though the competitor may feel he is concentrating and doing his best during practice, there seems to be a certain amount of isolation of self from the act . . . of having the *complete* being absent during the practice movements. It is as though one closes the door on totality, and only *partly* participates. Then when the *real* moment comes; when the ball must be rolled between the 1-3 pin, the performer brings a more complete effort to the performance. He is *all* there. He opens the door to *everything* as he combines inner and outer forces to accomplish *more* than he accomplished in practice. He sees it as being "for real." It is no longer a moment of practice, but the thing he practiced *for*. There is a different type of existence as he throws the ball in actual competition. He looks at it differently and the perspective is different than that achieved during the "trial runs." He is now tied up with something beyond the finite. He has geared himself to the *whole* possibility . . . to his *entire* potential.

Seldom does an athlete reach the ability to bring this *allness* to the practice sessions as well as to the actual competition. Usually, it is the great athlete who has learned that competition is a "package deal," and that there is no real separation between the enjoyment of movement either during practice or during the real thing. Or else, a few have been driven to this completeness by external prodding. Some coaches have been able to exact as much, if not more, from their players during the practice sions as during the game.

The artificiality in sport is often a result of our judgement systems. To go through a specific routine mechanically and unfeelingly reinforces the *impersonal*. To think of scores and statistics as purely objective means of evaluating what has happened is to ignore the life forces and the human achievement going on. We must not rely on *It* evaluation alone or we lose what is obtainable through sport. When the performer remains open to his movements, and to his feelings, he goes beyond the objective and touches on the intimate. To do this, he must willingly come to the testing of the self. He must be ready for fulfilment or for defeat, for intimacy with the self does not guarantee victory . . . it only guarantees *knowing*.

Reality is found much more easily in pick-up games and "sand-lot" competition, than in highly developed athletic programs. In these games where one plays just to play, there is little pretense, little organization, and one is free to play as he is. There is no need to falsify the self since no one expects such an unorganized team to look organized or polished. One reacts according to the situation rather than to what he thinks he *should* react to because of preconceived images of perfection exemplified by professionals. True, there are cases where even this type of play is centered around imitation of "heroes," but not at the expense of reality. One seldom *really* believes he is John Unitas, or that he can fake with the same ease, especially when he has been smeared in the mud of the field consistently by several ragged but determined linemen.

To imagine one is what one is not, or to gear any part of the self toward something that is false, and that is not an authentic part of the self—whether it is movement, or thought—is to walk away from what one *really* is, and consequently, from what one could be. One walks away from *being* and embraces artificiality. The individual dares a great deal in sport when he honestly seeks the truth. It isn't easy to face the fact that everything you *thought* you believed in was wrong . . . maybe not in an ethical way . . . but in a *true* way. When the athlete faces what he *is* rather than what he *thinks* he is or what he would *like* to be, he has to let go of many things that he has considered to be important up to that point. When one accepts the truth, one may lose everything *but* truth. But it is in this truth that one finds an authentic existence . . . and this is truly *everything*.

80

The public is well aware that much of athletics is fake. For instance, there is the show put on by the Globetrotters and by professional wrestlers. There are many other more subtle things being faked in the sport world, however, and sometimes no one realizes the falseness of it. Some players pretend they enjoy their athletic participation when in actuality it is a real grind. Others go through the motions even when the "feel" is just not there. Terry Bradshaw described one of his moments like this:

It was like a different world out there. I was reading the defenses well. I never felt I was losing my poise. And yet I couldn't hit the side of a barn. I was yelling at the guys in the huddle like I always do, but it was what you'd call false chatter. I kept saying, "Let's go, let's go." But deep down I knew that we weren't going anyplace. (243, p. 63)

Courtesy of Clear Creek High School. John Burr, Photographer.

Another form of "faking it" goes on in Little Leagues. Kids *play* like big leaguers. They make all the moves, jumping about, hitting their hands into the glove, tilting their hats, hitching up their pants, etc., even though they understand little of the reason why they act like this, other than it seems to be the *thing to do* because the "pros" do it. They *copy* rather than *being*. Their game loses much of the spontaneity that games should have if there is to be real joy in it. *Imitation* is an insult to the self since one *really isn't*, but simply looks like he is.

So the athlete finds himself faced with deciding what type of role he will follow. This role can be a false one, mimicked after someone else or after the type of individual he would like to be . . . or it may be a *true* role, or what the athlete really is.

Unless a vital change has been made in the personality and character of the individual at a certain point in time, the role includes a pattern that is consistent with the athlete's goals. A player will not make decisions based on his goal one day, and then entirely irrelevant decisions the next day if he maintains the same goal. Once an individual has chosen a goal, he gears his decision-making toward this end. It is this need to make decisions that is an important aspect of sport. One must choose what one considers to be necessary. One must make decisions concerning values, choosing the higher value over the lesser value in reference to the desired outcome. And through choice, one *becomes*.

Each decision is based on a characteristic of the individual. Each choice is based on choices that have been made before. As a result, one is not cut off from the past or from the future. The individual is a part of the present as a result of the past, and will be a part of the future because of the choices of the present. Once man chooses a goal, he must enter into decision-making in order to obtain it; therefore, he can no longer drift. He must make a stand and must base this stand on what he *is* and in reference to what he *wants*. Man's ends cannot be isolated from man's being. Otherwise, what he is, is false. In choosing, he moulds his ends out of what he is.

The enlightening, but sometimes frightening thing, about competition is that during the heat of the match or game, the individual many times finds he is not what he has always thought he was. In these moments, the athlete finds out what he or she *really* is, for it is hard to play a role under stress. It is hard to keep your cool in a panicky situation unless you actually *are* cool. It is hard to be honest when the outcome of the game depends on it unless you *really* are honest. So the athlete must many times look at the self as one is, whether he likes what he sees or not. It is immaterial. He *is* there.

Being, Awareness, and Selfhood

So one is not always what one thinks he is. The young girl on an elementary school team may play basketball, but she may not be a basketball player. The young man might pretend he is a professional football player, but in reality, he is not a professional.

One might assume from the above, that the being is partly what one *does*, not totally what one thinks. Yet, by virtue of continual thought, the being in reality may be one thing while *wishing* it were another . . . and by the thought process might develop from its moment of *not being*, to being. St. Augustine said: "No more than there is anyone who does not wish to be happy is there anyone who does not wish to be . . . "

But at any particular point in time, personal awareness is a combination of what *is* and what one *could be*. Reality itself, is what *is*. Reality, at the time, is the elementary school girl *playing* at being a basketball player and the young man *pretending* he is a professional football player. Yet, by virtue of these desires to be, one *becomes* over a period of time. "The human being cannot live in a condition of emptiness for very long: if he is not growing *toward* something, he does not merely stagnate; the pent-up potentialities turn into morbidity and despair, and eventually into destructive activities." (123, p. 22)

All who wish for certain goals do not attain them. The young man may make the college team but never make it to the professional league . . . yet, he has gone *beyond* the point he in reality *was* while pretending he was a pro. So he has become *more* than he was even though not becoming all he would have liked to be. So sport gives one a space and tools for being and becoming. It brings together the actuality of the person, and the action necessary to *be* more.

While participating in sport, one cannot help but be con-

83

scious of the body. The athlete knows that his performance depends on the readiness of his body. He eats a balanced diet; he gets plenty of sleep and rest; he exercises and practices faithfully . . . all to prepare his body for the contest. But it is during the actual movement that he becomes aware of his complete dependence on his body. It is his body that soars through the air for a rebound. It is his body that chases the softball; it is his or her body that sprints down the track in the dash. The body becomes the means for achieving purpose, belonging uniquely to the individual, and allowing him to perform the wishes of the mind and soul. In action, he becomes conscious of the self through the body. *He* reacts *through* the body. He jumps *with* the body. He runs *in* the body. It becomes *my* body that is propelled into the air. It is *my* body that must perform. It is *my* body that controls objects in the attempt to gain victory.

One knows more and more of the *me* as one becomes more and more aware of the body within which the *me* exists. It is this body that floats through the water. It is this body that moves over the high bar; it is this body that moves other bodies in going toward the goal posts in football. It is *my* body that runs, and jumps, and reacts.

During the events, the athlete consciously focuses on the objective to be gained. For some it is a record, for others a certain distance to be run within a certain length of time, for others a certain distance to jump. But though the focus is consciously on an external mark, the subconscious is focused on the body. The athlete is gathering together for the long jump, or tensing up the muscles for the upward leap over the high bar, or bringing the racket forward with the power of the arm and body. The act itself is in the *body*, not in the objective. He can perceive the objective, but the body must *do* it. Therefore, it becomes my body that plays, that eats, that sleeps. It is a *personal* body lived in only by me.

When the athlete is conscious of his body in totality, he begins to have a fuller picture of himself. He does not think of parts of himself as being isolated from his being. His foot is not separate from his leg, nor his hand from his arm. All of his parts are but pieces of a whole that is *his* body. In the same way, he does not think of his emotions or thoughts as being isolated

84

from his body . . . they do not drift and materialize on their own, but are *his* thoughts and *his* emotions. They belong to him just as his bodily parts.

It is impossible to separate the identity (the "I") of the athlete from the body. It is *my* finger that hurts when I jam it; it is *I* that must play with this jammed finger that hurts. *I* am the one that gets knocked down on a rebound, not just a body. Sometimes, one tries to forget this injury or "thorn in the side" in order to concentrate more on the action. For instance, the connection is treated as being impersonal by thinking and speaking of the injury as an "it." *It* still hurts, but I can play with it. *It* may handicap my shooting ability, but I can still do the job. But even in this connotation, one cannot sever the tie that connects the injured part to the totality of the individual. Even though the finger may be injured, it cannot be left behind. *It* must go where *I* go, and whether I can adjust to the fact that it is there is strictly up to me. But it is still my finger. So whether in sickness or in health, I am the body, and the body is me. I exist because of it.

But even though the body and the mind belong to me in reality, errors and mistakes inconsistent with the concept of the self are sometimes denied ("this can't happen to me"), and at other times are displaced from the self because the individual cannot accept the blunders of the self . . . "You are lousy today"; "You sure goofed that one." It is not the "I" that is playing lousy or that "goofed" the shot . . . it is the "you" in an attempt to disconnect the blame from the *being* that is threatened. One cannot conceive that he could do such a stupid thing; therefore, he denies it as being *him* by referring to himself in the second person rather than the first person. "*You* blew it." The error is no longer so *personal.*

One learns to know the body as it moves, not only that which is the body, but also objects and things the body comes in contact with. Objects around the individual become a part of the body's living, being used in many cases as an extension of the body and yet never being *the* body. "When he was finishing with a horse he was always *with* the horse, always in perfect motion with his horse. . . . " (197, p. 23)

The individual becomes aware of the senses of the body as it brings into play the non-living and non-personal objects around him, giving them to a certain extent a touch of life by the sensitivity of his body to them.

One does not automatically *know* what and whom one is competing against. When a girl steps up to the tee in a golf tournament, she does not feel a personal relationship to the other golfing contestants, nor is she conscious of the *real* being of the other girls. *Appearances* come to the individual at first. Then according to *how* one looks at what appears to be, that object is then accepted as *being* a specific thing. The shape of an ink spot might appear to be a bird to an individual, but realizing it is just ink on paper, the individual perceives the object to be what it *is*, ink on paper. As man perceives things, he becomes more and more involved with things; consequently, things become a *part of him*. And as he allows things to come into contact with *his* world, they become a part of his awareness . . . as a result they have *meaning* to him. He doesn't necessarily *know* that which he perceives even at this point, but he is *open* to it, and what he is open to is *real* to him. Through his perception and his awareness, he builds his existence within *reality*. What he experiences is a confrontation with his being. He *exists*, and what he is competing against exists, and as a result he is placed up against reality by his involvement in sport. And in his existence, he lives as a *total* being, sensing and touching upon other parts of the *complete* world which surrounds him. There is no separation in his being of emotions and physical reactions . . . every part of him is a part of him. Nothing can be isolated that exists *within* his being, nor can the world *without* his being be isolated. What he *feels* and what he *is* and what he is in contact *with*, are all one thing.

What man perceives in the sport situation is dependent upon how man sees himself. Out of all the factors revolving around him, he selects what he thinks is *relevant* to him. When Chip Oliver left professional football to become a hippie, this is what he said: "Football is a silly game. It's irrelevant and I don't need it anymore." (169, p. 21)

Space, movement, sound, senses, sight, etc. play different roles in the athlete's perception. One day the sound of the crowd might be exhilarating; the next it might be depressing . . . dependent on how he feels he is playing and contributing at that point in time. Many athletes learn to shut out distracting elements, such as the sounds of the crowd. One might say that when man perceives, he *chooses* what he wishes to exist in *his* world regardless of what exists in the total world around him. Everything still exists, but only chosen things exist in *his* sphere of action.

All that is actually present in sport gives the individual material he can build from in order to obtain meaning in *his* world. After watching Torben Ulrich play tennis, Mark Kram described him in this way:

> The peripheral things do not move him. He continues to play because the game, like jazz, has become an extension of himself, a thing vital to the understanding of his self. Then there is the feel of the game that he is always so conscious of: the sweet percussion of ball and gut, the beautiful flow and pattern whan a point is played out to the full. . . . He plays a game within a game according to rules he alone understands, to a tune he alone is hearing. . . . He becomes a part of the game, not a disruptive part, but a part almost like the ball, moving as gracefully, as predictably as the movements of a piece of music. (108, p. 84)

The athlete is open to *all* of it, but he *selects* that which seems useful and meaningful to him, and becomes a part of it. He builds according to the dimensions of his own being, choosing that which gives his being *reality*. What the individual *feels is real* to him, *is* real to him. What he *senses* by his emotions and feelings is just as real as the opponent across the tennis net. The wind he fights on the curve is real, just as the discus he projects into the air is real. What he imagines in his mind can also be real, depending on how strongly he *believes* in its reality.

But what is real to one may not be to another. One man may be so mentally tied up in his pain that he does not even feel the wind on the curves. For the man, the wind is *not real*. To understand what the athlete perceives as real and what has meaning for him as an individual, we would have to feel as he feels—to see as he sees. To exist as he exists, we would have to be *aware* of what he is aware of. What a man *is* comes from what a man is *open* to. Reality, to any one individual, is what one *perceives* to be reality.

The athlete becomes free through the perception of the self and the situation, *if* it is a true perception. Just because we might *think* something is such and such a way, it is not that way unless it *is*, although in our perceptions it *seems* real to us. To see the self and situation as it is, the experience must be first-hand. It is the performer who is involved in the movement and the thought processes during the action of the competition; therefore, what happens during the involvement happens *only* to the performer. It is his moment . . . it is his action . . . consequently, it is his responsibility and his opportunity to find the self, and through the discovery, to achieve *his* potential. The spectator may be completely involved in *watching* the performance. He may sense the tremendous effort and sacrifice through vicarious involvement, but watching is not an *actual* part of the action. For the spectator to feel what the athlete feels, he would have to be involved physically, mentally, and emotionally, in the *very* same way. One affirms oneself *by being there*— by being in the midst of the action—not just by identifying with someone who *is* there. Again, Chip Oliver put his finger on the problem when he made this statement: "I would look up at the people in the coliseum and realized I wasn't helping them. . . . All we're doing in professional football is entertaining these people and they don't need to be entertained. They need to do their *own* [italics mine] creative thing." (169, p. 21)

But even though the athlete is there, he rarely understands what is happening to him. He knows that at times there is a discontent he cannot explain; there is an uneasiness with the self that he finds hard to live with. He is involved physically in the activity, and yet in the back of his physical commitment, there is something more. Sometimes, it can be explained rationally. Other times, there is no reasonable explanation. Man often becomes more and more involved, being more and more aware there is *something* there, but not knowing what. Tom Koch said, "I was always trying to get in the match. You need something to get going and I never got a break. It was one of those days. You are out there waiting and waiting and waiting, and all of the sudden it is all over." (79, p. 15)

Courtesy of Clear Creek High School.

The athlete feels "right," or he doesn't. He acts; his body and his mind responds to a given situation, and the *action* he is involved in holds a meaning that he cannot define in words. But as he continually joins in the action, he realizes more and more that he is becoming open to *that something* . . . and as the integration takes place, he begins to see himself. "And right there, when you pick up that weight, your life expands. Your whole life passes before you," said George Frenn. (167, p. 55) The more true and authentic his involvement and commitment to his actions in sport, the more quality there seems to be to his awareness of himself and his being—for his being is relative to his commitment. He not only exists, he exists in a way that is progressively being developed. He becomes a part of a formulative process.

When this *being* is fully caught in a moment of competition, it is as if everything is focused on a *oneness* that flows. There seems to be a power present that allows the individual to "walk on water," or to create miracles in those precious moments of pure ecstasy. He runs and jumps and *lives* through the pure play process, which is composed of joy and pleasure and exuberance and laughter; even the pain seems completely tolerable in these few precious and rare moments of *being*, and of knowing that one is just that . . . a oneness and a wholeness. Some athletes express this feeling as having "been my day," or in the thought "I could have shot with my eyes closed and it would have dropped in," or "I couldn't have missed if I had wanted to." But words are never sufficient to express the feeling—it is an unexpressible joy. Though rarely coming in purity, it is enough to send the athlete back again and again to competition.

So sport has many dimensions. There is sport as the spectator sees it. There is sport as the performer sees it. And there is sport as sport *is*. The *allness* of a certain act such as the pole vault, can never be seen in its entirety by a spectator. Taking part in the act is purely a personal matter. One cannot truly experience what the performer is experiencing by simply watching. But the real truth of that movement high into the air may not even be completely known by the performer himself. He utilizes scientific knowledge to perform the movements as he should to attain the most height. He also utilizes practical knowledge when he goes beyond the scientific and touches on *personal* experience, and *senses* when the time has come to make the lifting effort. He "feels" the pole and his body in relation to the pole and bar. He "senses" what movements he must make to get over that obstacle. But even beyond this, there is a moment outside of the scientific and the empirical. He *hopes* for the miracle that will take him over. There is a reaching for something more than he can experience or know up to that point. This entire experience of being suspended in time and air is a personal matter that demands *intimacy*. No one else, not even another performer, can enter entirely into this moment.

But one does not just "feel" as one competes. One also analyzes and rationalizes, and *thinks out* solutions. Subjective and objective awareness is important in development of the

90

being and in its performance. The self is *both* personal and impersonal. Parts of it one knows as being *me*. Other parts are as a stranger, unknown and untried.

But there is more than *just* the body. There is the mind, and the emotions, and the many other facets of the individual that exists *in* and *is* the body. The athlete is forever involved in strategy. He continually *thinks* of the upcoming games, the pending events. He analyzes, he rationalizes, he uses his mental attributes along with his phsyical skills. The athlete is also emotionally involved. He feels and reacts and laughs and cries. He becomes angry and kind; he feels closeness and isolation. He *responds* emotionally to all the many stimuli existing in his world. But there is another type of awareness. Many over the years have called this the spiritual side of man, but regardless of the terminology, there does exist an area beyond the body and the mind and the emotions. It cannot be defined concretely and it cannot be measured . . . but it seems to be in this area that the *something* reaches out to such heights of greatness. We speak of "being up" for the game; of having a "psychological edge," of "being high enough to fly a kite." Part of this is mental, but most of it is not controlled by conscious thought. And one can never predict when or where it will occur . . . but oftentimes, there are unexpected miracles as a result. One *glides* through the action as though one is in a different world. A writer's description of Joe Namath tries to explain a great night: "Moving with a detached gracefulness, Namath will usually give the vague impression that he is somehow removed from the grimy infighting of the other 21 men on the field." (143, p. 57)

One does fantastic things as though they were everyday accomplishments. Everything . . . the mental, the physical, the emotional, and that *something* . . . clicks. At times, it becomes almost a mystical experience as one seems to transcend what one *usually* is. After setting world records in the 100-yard dash and in the 200, Chi Cheng said: "I didn't feel like I did it. I felt like someone else ran, not me." (227, p. 48) It is as though the body and mind and emotions are in contact with a source of unlimited power . . . and one is, if one believes in God. "But when he, too, who abhors the name, and believes himself to be godless, gives his whole being to addressing the *Thou* of his life, as a *Thou* that cannot be limited by another, he addresses God." (29, p. 76)

This feeling has a needed core of quietness for the dedicated athlete. When one competes, one is surrounded by the outside world. And usually, where there is competition, there is the noise of the crowd that comes to watch. But beyond the noise of spectators at an athletic event, there is the sound of silence within the athlete. One can *feel* it within the concentration of the performer. As the action gets longer and harder, it is the *me* that breathes hard, that seeks a rest, that searches for a dignified finish to the fatigue. It's *me* that listens to the sounds of the crowd, or who cuts the noise off from my own private world. And just as it is the *me* that does the work and enters into the performance, it is the *me* that seeks the solitude of silence for the preparation preceding the event. *I* go into my inner shell to listen to my own voices, which really has nothing to do with the noise *outside* of myself.

Courtesy of Brevard College.

Sometimes, even the crowd has its own sense of silence. This silence may seem to be a *void*, but it is much more than that. It is a moment when *importance* is prerequisite over sound. It is a time when physical or verbal expression is not adequate. It is a point in space and time that is precious and even awesome in a way. It is during the silence that everything has intensified, and the *mental self* is crucial to the performance. "New York basketball had been an emotional, communal phenomenon all year as the players interracted with one another and with the crowd to produce an intensity of experience rarely felt in any sport." (240, p. 93)

This silence can be seen preceding any athletic event. Each individual becomes lost in his or her own thoughts—the "getting up" for the game—the "getting ready" for the effort to prove his or her ability against the opponent.

Many turn away from this silence because it is a lonely time, and in many ways it is a time of discomfort because of the intensity of concentration and thought. It is much easier to just walk away from the silence and to bury it under noise and activity. But it is within this silence that one thinks about things that are *really* relevant. The athlete knows that soon he will be *tested*—and everything is geared toward this time of testing. He hopes he will prove capable, but he doesn't *know* he will. During this time of silence, one is no longer looking forward to the event tomorrow . . . it is *now* . . . one is about to be in the very midst of the action, and if he is to survive it with dignity, he must put his doubts and fears in place to prepare himself for the competition.

> Outwardly I probably appeared calm but inside me a volcano of nervous energy was slowly turning over. One moment I was full of doubts—doubting my own ability, my fitness and my purpose. Then I would reassure myself that I was capable of beating my opponents, analyzing and comparing their past performances with my own. (49, p. 22)

What the athlete does or does not do depends only on himself and how he has prepared himself to respond, and he knows it. He is at a point where he must confront himself and his environment and his opponent . . . all at the same time. The silence brings with it this fact, and the fact that he does exist in the midst of this challenge . . . and the only way to prove himself is to meet the challenge. The silence does not necessarily bring with it the sense of readiness or ability to meet the challenge *well*. It simply signifies that one is conscious that one is *there* to be challenged. One exists regardless of the outcome . . . one is geared through his being to recognize that *this is it*. One no longer prepares, or walks away from it, or dreams about it. One is *now* surrounded by it, and as such *one is whatever one proves himself to be*. As Kipchoge Keino from Kenya said: "I feel when I go to run in a race my main ambition is to take part in the competition. *The race is there* [italics mine]." (140, p. 22)

So it is through the self—through self-awareness, at this point in time, that one has the potential for meaning within the realm of competition. It doesn't mean the individual will find meaning in the confrontation . . . it does not even mean the individual will look for it or be aware it is there. But regardless, the *potential* remains.

What the potential is, is relative to the athlete. Each athlete has a chance for a personal meaning that is unique and meaningful only to that *one* individual. "Every organism has one and only one central need in life, to fulfil its own potentialities." (123, p. 81) It is the potential for the meaning to *his* or *her* being, to *his* or *her* unification, to *his* or *her* accomplishment, to *his* or *her* self. The athlete *may* find the potential if he is open to it. Perhaps, the not knowing if he will find *his* potential and *his* meaning and *his* victory is what intensifies the silence preceding or during the actual competition.

For one probably senses that sport does not necessarily, and probably rarely, *cause* the individual to find himself. If anything, it makes it harder because of the continuous action, emotion, and stress. It merely *allows* him to look for himself through an awareness of the possibilities and the potential concentrated in his selfhood. Consequently, sport offers challenge and threat, security and insecurity. However, it's true that during play, most athletes never concern themselves with philosophical questions concerning their participation in competition, although some do ask themselves questions of why and how, which do border on the philosophical. For instance, why do I love to jump, or to swim, or to run? What is it about this particular sport that gives me moments of elation? Is it worth it? But sometimes, the questions are asked even though one may not realize he is asking about his existence and his involvement . . . and it is at these *sometimes* that one reaches elation as one touches on the meaning of one's existence.

If one can find meaning anywhere in life, then the sports arena *should* be the place. *So much* goes on there. *So much* is involved there. *So much* is committed there. But for most, it is simply a battlefield and a place of conflict for this is what our society has thrived on. Messersmith, a professional pitcher, says: "It's the emotional feeling—the highs and lows—that you don't get out of anything else. It's conflict, a war, a battle; a very complex feeling." (17, p. 24) Jimmy Jacobs described the great handball player, Paul Haber, in this way: "When Paul is in there, he's in a war. He hangs his emotional hat on that ball. It's all he has in life. Handball." (244, p. 30)

So how does man come to grips with himself and his environment without having the values of his society dictate what he will be and how he will react? How does man find out who he is while being involved in endless struggles and varied events? How does one "find himself" in the world of sport when everything about him would tear him apart and defeat him?

There is no easy answer, but one thing sport has going for it is that athletics allows the individual to bring his own unique *person* into play. It demands *all* of him during the participation, not just the physical or the mental or the emotional. At the same time, there is pressure from the collective body forcing one toward socialization and sacrifice of *the* self. Yet, it is the *individual* that participates and that makes the final decisions concerning himself. It is *I* who chooses who I am. It is *me* who is tested.

So as the person becomes involved, there is a growth and a change going on *inside* the person, as well as the development of *outward* skills. The athlete faces himself under many and various situations, and in this confrontation with self, he becomes aware that he *is*, and since he *is*, he is responsible to *what* he is. In this recognition of the value of self, he accepts the value of the life of others, for if his life is of importance to him, then the life of others also holds importance. By accepting the value of his individualism, he turns his back on the claims others might have on his soul. " . . . The self is always born and grows in interpersonal relationships. But no 'ego' moves on into responsible selfhood if it remains chiefly the reflection of the social context around it." (123, p. 77) Consequently, the individual does not see his being as belonging to society, but to himself. Perhaps this is what led Schollander to say: "I don't have any responsibility to an audience. I don't believe any amateur athlete has. We are here to perform for our pleasure." (181, p. 33) The importance of an athlete's life force is not dependent on the emphasis society places upon it because of society's values . . . but is dependent purely on the importance he sees in his own being. He *is*, and it is enough.

Sports, as we know them today, do reach out for the soul of the man in many instances, as they demand that he be a social and a sacrificing being. Sport asks that men be something they cannot be authentically, for no man who values his life will give it away to something that has less value. True, athletes do reach a plateau in their lives where they can *willingly* work with others in what is commonly called "teamwork." Yet, they are not *giving* themselves to the team; they are contributing in a way that is beneficial to themselves and to others making up the group. The athlete is not allowing himself to be lost in the mass as much as he is helping others reach a goal of common interest. Even though it is said that *the team* wins or loses, he maintains his identity aside and apart from the collective unit. He is a "team player" because he *contributes* to the whole; not because he is *owned* by the whole. There is a big difference. What one experiences while participating in sport is an individual thing, even though one might be competing on a team. Two people may not come across the same "happening." There are some things that are consistent, and would remain as such regardless of the way the individual views it. For instance, the tennis net is a regulation height. The tennis ball meets certain specifications. The boundary lines cover the same area on every regulation court. Yet, even these things might be viewed differently by individuals. The court and the space to be covered might look much larger to the short, small individual, than to the tall, lanky person. But outside of the regulation boundaries, equipment, etc., each thing is unique to the individual as far as experiences. These experiences are viewed in the light of emotions, desires, motivation, goals, etc.

The actual experience of life becomes intensified in sport. One is more aware of what is happening as one moves and is moved upon. There are extremes of joy and sorrow, pain and pleasure, etc. One becomes more *sensitive* to what one is and to what one is experiencing. It is as though the fatigue and the exertion open doors that allow one to see things in a fuller—but still an individual—perspective.

What one finds out about himself is relative to the situation. And within this discovery, freedom of choice aids the discovery. One realizes the self by what one does, what one feels, what one senses, what one thinks. Some of this is outside the realm of choice, and as such, has no bearing except as it is based on *previous* choice.

As one makes his own individual choices, one learns to know his self through the experience in specific activities. He *exists* in the long jump. He *is* during the spike in volleyball. He *acknowledges* the missed putt and the part *he* played in the miscalculation. *I* jumped. *I* spiked. *I* putted. It was *I* that perceived the space and the ball and the body. The spectator may have watched me do it, but it was *I* that was involved. I *did* it, and as such I have the responsibility for the results. I made the choice, not my parents, not the society in which I live ... but *me* ... and as such I have experienced self within a specific situation. I have affirmed that I am. *I have been there.*

But even though the athlete has been there, or is there—there are times when the athlete consciously becomes *detached* from his actions. It *seems* he is no longer there. The basketball player releases the ball and holds the follow-through as his conscious self gives way to the flight of the ball into the air and through the goal. He *sees* the ball and loses concept of the self. And yet, though he does not *seem* to be there, he is very much so. The situation could not exist without his *thereness*. The ball could not have been released into the air without his being there. He is a part of the happenings even though he has become detached from the action after the release.

The highly competitive individual becomes amazed at his lack of importance in the scheme of things at times. At a crucial point in the game, the athlete notices insignificant things: a crack in the floor, a piece of gum on the wall, a dirty spot on a tennis shoe. It is as though outside circumstances have been magnified, while individual identity has temporarily been lost in the madness of the moment. He is there, and yet he "seems out of it." The reality he perceives has gone beyond the self. He has transcended his individual identity to become a part of the whole of reality around him.

Emotions are not isolated from the participant; they are just a part of the *whole,* just as the crack and gum and spot of dirt are a part of the whole. The emotions are *there* because they are experienced. When a player has been submerged in the total involvement of sport . . . when he has been in the middle of *it* . . . when he has performed as well as possible and has known the best he can do—then sport is not meaningless or insignificant. It seems to justify what one has been through to take part. The sweat, the tears, the joy, the pain—they become a justified part of existence because he has been *where it all is,* and they were necessary in the process. He has taken part . . . and as a result, *he* is a part.

It was *he alone* that felt seams on the ball. It was he who perceived it in his hand. It was he who took one moment in time and made it all his as *he* reacted to the stimuli within that point in time and space. What the athlete experiences is a private feeling. What happens to me as I touch the leather of a basketball and as my mind sends signals through my body as to how to react to this leather is a moment that cannot be shared with another in totality . . . this is *my* moment of being . . . of feeling . . . of responding. This is my own private world within the world. Others can experience what I am experiencing *indirectly* by watching—but the experience itself is all *mine,* for it is *my* hand on the ball.

It is within this private world that one expresses his inner thoughts and feelings. One *projects* what one feels into action.

One feels aggression, so one becomes aggressive during the action. One feels like playing, so one *plays*. However, our training in what society expects of us as individuals does inhibit the individual on the athletic field just as it does elsewhere. Just because one feels like hitting an opponent, one does not necessarily hit him. But the feeling can still be *expressed*, even though indirectly. One *beats* the opponent scorewise, rather than physically.

There is a tremendous amount of frustration in sport. George Frenn said, "I want to start slowly . . . when I start off badly I go all the way. It's like falling off a cliff." (167, p. 55) Because of the "conflict of interest" present in sport, one finds many of his goals blocked as he competes against others for the same goal. As a result, it is not an easy thing to have self-control when one must hold back because of the pressure exerted during competition. There is continual conflict between desire and actual achievement. Yet, even greater than controlling the conflict, would be the ability to understand the self and to integrate the self with the goals being sought in such a way that no conflict results. Conflict is very seldom external, but is usually an internal thing. Therefore, an internal knowledge could avoid many problems of conflict. But it's not nearly as easy as it sounds.

What we feel and think is often symbolic, and does not always represent what we *think* it does . . . nor does the symbol always have a meaning to us. What man symbolizes through thought and what he *experiences* needs to maintain a working relationship that is meaningful if the athlete is to. reach his potential. The complex thought process with its symbolization enters into sport just as surely as the physical processes with its biological changes.

If what is happening in sport *has no symbolic meaning* to the athlete, then this individual misses out on the *realness* possible in the complexity of sport and man. The relationship of sport and man is authentic only when one becomes a part of the other. The *man thinks*, and *sport is*, and between the two there is a *relation* that has intimate and personal meaning.

Thought without meaning becomes a mechanical process, and the individual reverts to animal instinct and biological func-

Courtesy of Brevard College.

tions. Without the *feeling* for what is happening in the sport environment, there is no relation. One feels many things when one mentions the name of the sport one is engaged in if one has a relation of meaning with this sport. One *feels pride* when one mentions defense if one plays good defense on a basketball team. There is a bond that connects the individual to the action. Engagement in *his* sport is where it is at. He is a part of the thing that makes him *feel;* that makes him *exist;* that makes him *live.* What happens to him as a result of sport is not something that can be described in words, but it happens just the same. Mario Andretti tried to explain what racing meant to him in these words: "Why do I race? . . . I don't think anybody except me can understand it. . . . I would give up everything—my home, my family, everything I've gained—to stay in racing." (34, p. 46) Man associates what he feels *symbolically.*

In any sport, man lives on the edge of human experi-

100

ence. The thrill of movement and sense of competition keeps man *attentive* as he precariously balances on this edge of the totality of experiences. (202, p. 97)

Symbolically, or otherwise, sport appeals to many facets of man. The violence and the physical contact touch the animal within the man. The beauty and the graceful rhythm touch the aesthetic in the individual. The moments of supreme awe bring with them a sense of the religious, while the chance for brotherhood appeals to the humaneness in man.

Integrating these many sides of man is not easy in sport. If anything, the athletic field might be the hardest place to *be human,* to feel toward others, to respect the self. "There are other factors tending to destroy sport: too much money, too much pressure, too much exposure. The total influence of them all is to fix games, to remove the fundamental drama, the mystery and the art of sport by *dehumanizing it* [italics mine]." (69, p. 35)

Winning is not geared toward loving. It is based on defeat and conquering and achieving . . . all at the expense of the opponent. One cannot turn from hate to love or from violence to peace at will. One cannot be a conqueror one moment and a brother the next if the basic philosophy is one of *defeating.*

Sport is absurd when man looks for social benefits *without* understanding what is really going on. Trying to *beat* an opponent scorewise does not lead to cooperative or empathic actions. The way sport is geared toward *defeating* makes it almost impossible for the individual to *help* him at the same time. Yet, the possibilities are there when one realizes there is *more* than winning to the game. There is a *being* . . . a *thereness* . . . an *involvement* . . . and a sense of *love* in the relationship. These things are not dependent on winning or losing, but only on *awareness.* When one becomes aware of the self, one begins to see and to be aware of *others.* In order for sport to offer a human experience, the player cannot be forgotten, whether teammate or opponent, but he must be *felt* . . . or more specifically, *felt for.*

There are two worlds, or ways of looking at the world,

of entering into relationship with it, depending on the spirit in which we approach it. We may see in it nothing but things, mechanisms, from those of physics to those of biology and even of psychology. Art, philosophy, religion can also become things, collections of concepts, formulae, definitions. On the other hand, one can lay oneself open to the world of persons, awaken to the sense of the person. By becoming oneself a person one discovers other persons round about, and one seeks to establish a personal bond with them. (217, p. 179)

To really feel for the self, or for others, one must understand the difference between existence and essence. One exists before he actually takes part in an activity such as sport. But once he becomes involved, *really* involved, the athlete finds himself open to self-actualization and a sense of humaneness as he reaches for that "something" that gives him meaning on the athletic field. His external existence becomes lost in the search for an internal existence that takes in the important elements of life. The way he performs becomes more than a matter of skill and winning. He performs to reach a realm of *valid* being, for he knows that one can exist and still not be. There is a supreme emptiness when one simply is present, and there is nothing more. The athlete knows that he can exist in a nothingness although his body moves and breathes. But where there is essence, he *is*. There is more than mere existence. There is an openness to life ... a potential for valid purpose ... for an authentic life. He exists in an *important* way. The athlete is no longer simply *there,* but he is *involved.* The speed driver with essence no longer merely rides in his high-powered car. He *races* in it.

This awareness of the self as *being* is beautifully described by Jo Ann Houts:

It was the third game that I had pitched that day. I did not think I could last through another game, but suddenly I was overcome by a power that rendered me capable to pitch forever. I lost the immediate awareness of my team around me. It was just me, *alone,* on the mound grasping at a round, weightless orb. I became extremely sensitive to the motions of my body. The minute muscles in my fingers were waiting for the signal to release their power and force; I could feel my whole body moving through the air, transcending all barriers; I could feel the initial thrust as all my body force was extended with the pitched ball.

But suddenly there came a moment of doubt. I felt that I was entangled in a silly, nonsense game with myself. After all, as soon as my acts were over, I would have to prove myself anew with each pitch, with each new play in the game. It was a never-ending entanglement, to prove with each move that I *was* my act. For a second fear gripped at me, pulling and pushing at the very core of my existence. What if I did not get another chance? What if this was it? The recognition of my own finitude had come about in my sport experience. The realization of death existed for me, in only a flash, and then it was gone. Why it had come, I do not know, but to feel so small, there on the mound, alone, in the midst of a tied ball game, was it the realization of the death of the game, or of me, through which the game existed?

My body continued to move and perform its function while my mind was caught in turmoil. The game did not seem to be going fast enough, yet I was lagging behind it.

Then I saw the ball reach its intended target. The pitch felt like a unique extension of my whole self, with the ball not to be touched by the "object" standing at home plate. Vaguely, I heard the umpire call "Strike!" It gave me a feeling as though I had made a safe but daring journey through unknown territories, breathing ultimate freedom at last. Freedom! I had transcended my environment. I was my act in sport and nothing more, nothing less. I felt my *authentic* being. I was aware! I was feeling sport! The honest effort and the complexity of my seemingly simple movements made my body, my mind, and my soul seem to reflect beauty and truth of a living, involved human being in sport.

Then the next pitch had to be thrown. I was trying hard to maintain my joy. All of a sudden the game was over.

The opponents came into view. They were happy, scream-
ing, throwing gloves into the air. The realization of the
moment had come to me. I knew what I had done. The
game was tied in the last inning; there were two outs, the
bases were loaded. The count on the batter was three balls,
two strikes. Yes, in my joy, in my transcendence of the
situation, I had walked in the winning run. It was over.
How absurd! Gone as quickly as it had come. I realized
again how small I was among the complexities of life. The
game was over and I had to continue to be me through the
never ending responsibility of choices that shape my life. I
knew that in some small way I left this peak experience a
different person than when I entered the game. I was
changed. Some small part of my being had become more
total in its encounter with life." (245, p. 72)*

* Used with permission of Jo Ann Houts and the *Journal of Health,
Physical Education, and Recreation.*

Chapter 5

SPORT AND I-THOU RELATIONSHIPS

If one believes in an integrated and a working relationship between the conscious and the unconscious, or between the mental and the physical being, one wonders how integration is ever accomplished in the sports world because of the many things going on during sports action which creates division, rather than integration. The mind is concentrated on external objectives such as sending the shuttlecock over the net, or chasing down a tennis ball to return it to the opponent.

The athlete is continually focusing his attention to outside forces and objects. In this focusing of attention on external environment, we find the individual in a state of non-being in a sense, for the self exists only in relation to what it can *do* to external stimuli and objects. Yet, at the same time, the self is being acted upon by the simple act of concentration and goal orientation. In the words of Torben Ulrich, "The match completely takes me over. If I am in my groove, the ball will take care of itself, and my movements and thoughts and concentration will be determined and conducted by the ball, not by me. The same is true of music. It is the thing—music, ball—which is the doer, not the person." (108, pp. 84-86) The being is concentrated and finely tuned in order to cope with the external. Consequently, the being finds a point of integration as the mental and the physical combine to accomplish the acts that the being is focusing on.

Because of the extensive use of objects in sport, many athletes become "hung up" with the importance of these objects. Part of this may stem from the fact that objects in sport are more than they *seem*. The basketball might be described, but when thought of by the athlete it becomes much more than the description indicates . . . it's to be passed and dribbled, and shot. Although only an object, it becomes a means of involvement for man in a world of movement and emotion and reality. The ball, however, means something different to each individual who handles it. The player "plays" with it. The manager "cleans" it. The dog "chases" it. The manufacturer "produces" it.

At the same time, if one thinks of the basketball only in terms of what it is, then it is *nothing* but leather and air. But when one thinks of it in terms of what man can *do* with it, then it becomes *everything*. The object is given a life of its own by man's use of it. Man *relates* to the object because of his involvement with it. And in this relation there is a personal meaning, unique to each individual. The ball is a *nothing* until there is a *meeting* between it and man, then it becomes a part of life ... or more specifically, a part of the athlete's life with whom the object has become involved in a *living* and a *moving relationship*.

Courtesy of Clear Creek High School. Terry Muehr, Photographer.

But man must move beyond the objects in his world of

action. When the individual selects a particular sport, he accepts the limitations and advantages inherent in that sport. He accepts the legal tools or objects connected with the sport . . . specific size of the ball, specific height of the net, etc. Along with the acceptance of the rules and the instruments he is allowed to use, he must accept the boundaries of his own body. He must work within the limitations and advantages of his physical build, as well as within the parameters of his mental and emotional world. He takes what he has, 5'2" frame, 150 pounds, or whatever, and along with the objects connected to the specific sport, he uses his body and the allowable objects as instruments or tools to accomplish a given goal within the space dimensions. He takes part by the fact that he enters into the participation, but whether this participation leads to any type of meaning other than that of being there is solely dependent upon the individual's awareness of *why* he is participating.

Part of this awareness must be derived from the presence of others, either in reality or symbolically. Man is not totally alone even in individual sports, for even then he is working against what others have done in the event during their own "aloneness." He competes against records, against stars of past years, and against the norm or the par. So when the individual considers the reality of his being, he must consider it in the light of the reality of *others.* He compares his achievements *with* the achievement of others. He may be in a situation alone at a specific moment in space, but the totality of the moment holds meaning only in relationship with the totality of what others have achieved. So his being is tied up in a sense *with* the being of others.

Life, in many ways, is a process of osmosis. When one touches upon something in his life, he absorbs the experience and it becomes a part of himself. Sport is a place where two or more life forces can meet, and as a result, absorb something from each other. This absorption of life to life is one of the great potentials of action on the sports field. As life comes to grip with life, it becomes *the* thing of importance over and above the action going on during play. Sport no longer holds the same meaning to the individual when it moves from an impersonal experience to a humane confrontation. It changes from a thing of contention to a *vehicle* of knowing and sharing. It is a place where one meets another as a part of *all* life . . . where one is involved in a *real* action far beyond the superficial motions and goals of winning and defeating. It is simply the place where one can say "hello" to his fellow man *despite* the competitiveness involved. Phil Woolpert described this feeling of brotherhood when he told how Bill Russell reacted during a game in New Orleans at a time when segregation was still highly enforced, and racial tension was quite high:

The crowd cheered our Negroes kind of dutifully at the start, but you could almost bathe in the tension. About seven minutes into the game, a ball went up in the air and Russell came down with it. Two kids from Loyola fell, hard. Bill looked at them, then he put the ball down and helped both of them up. The crowd went wild, and the Negro kids on the team got standing ovations when they went out of the game that night. (95, p. 74)

Martin Buber emphasizes that the *relations* individuals have with other individuals are what is important. "For to step into pure relation is not to disregard everything but to see everything in the *Thou,* not to renounce the world but to establish it on its true basis." (29, pp. 78-79)

The athlete can have I-You relationships (impersonal individual-to-individual relationships), I-It relationships (individual-to-objects and impersonal things, such as wealth, success, etc.), or I-Thou relationships (personal and caring relationships).

Complete living results from what has been termed by Buber as I-Thou relationships . . . where there is a certain amount of love and caring present. Unless there is some kind of an empathy response to others, then competition is more of a mechanistic performance than a *human experience.*

The *Thou* speaks of a kind of reverence and respect for the living part of the other one meets. Martin Buber emphasizes the word *Thou* rather than the second person word "you." He does so because the word *Thou* means "loved-one," and is not impersonal as the word "you." In this way, he stresses that the relationship between the *I* and the *Thou* is a connection of intimacy brought about by a bond of love. The *I* develops through its commitment to another, for to be human, and to compete in a humane way, one must be aware of the importance of relationships with other people. These relationships must be based on *realness,* not on superficial or artificial bonds. The person must *truly* feel for and care for the people around him. By having relationships *with* others, or by recognizing the *Thou,* one reaffirms the *I* of the self.

Many individuals compete only with an I-You or I-It sense. There is no real feeling for the opponent. While a few athletes play *with* others, there are some who always play *against* others, or whose only goal is to *conquer,* to *win,* to *defeat,* to *beat,* those opposing them. There is no humaneness in the play . . . it is like a business, with no room for intimacy. The word we commonly hear to describe this type of action is that "he killed me," or "he wiped me off the courts," or "he never knew I was even there."

This lack of concern for the opponent is shown in what Buber calls an I-It relationship. Everything during the competition holds an impersonal and institutionalized meaning . . . there is no closeness, no empathy. It is as though the athlete were competing against an object rather than a person or a human being. This I-It world is a necessary world, as man must live with materialism, and institutions, and objects of all kinds. Yet, when this relationship to unliving things, the *its,* is carried over to living beings in activities such as competition, the *I* loses its chance for authentic meaning. The *I* cuts itself off from *feeling,* from emotions that are *real.* It substitutes *non-feeling* for being. It sees potential *thous* only as *its,* and meaningfulness takes on a limited relationship. If the individual never goes beyond the I-It impersonal relations, he forfeits the development and growth that is rightfully his through openness. He takes on a false world and closes out an authentic existence.

As one plays, one tends to see the other player or the other team as moving figures that *look* a certain way. The opponent looks "sharp," or the other team looks "tall." What we are seeing is the body, or the outer appearance because we do not really *know* the other team or the other individual. We do not know what thoughts are passing through the other's mind, or what muscles are hurting him, or what anxieties he might be feeling concerning the competition. He simply looks like a strong competitor or weak opposition. We do not see the total man or the totality of the opponent, but only what he *appears* to be. To break it down, we are basically seeing the body, not the man. But it is this body we must manipulate or "beat" during the competition. Our success as athletes, depends on our ability to control the *other's* body as well as our own. We must make the opponent take his cut into the middle of the defense rather than along the baseline, even though what *he* really wants to do is drive down the baseline. But we are attempting to force his *body* inside regardless of where his *mind* tells him to go. We are concerned with the movements of the body, rather than specifically with the direction of the mind, for by forcing the body we deal with the mind. We *see* the body, not the mind. But once we lose sight of the body, then we have to directly deal with the mind . . . we must anticipate what the next mental move is in order to recover our direct relationship with the body. As a result, the opponent's body becomes an impersonal object or a *thing* to be manipulated, to be used as a means to our end. We feel good when we outmaneuver the opponent and send a backhand across court rather than down the line for the point. There is a certain amount of self satisfaction in "outthinking" the opponent. Although what we have seen in reality is not the mind as the maneuvered object, but the body.

At times, this satisfaction in controlling another person's body does bring a sense of guilt to the individual. He does not particularly feel good about running a lesser skilled player across the court time and time again for an easy point. He senses that although he is looking great in reference to this object he is controlling, there is *more* than the body before him. He begins to feel guilty because he is being selfish and is ignoring what he knows must be going on *within* the body before him. He too has been controlled and soundly beaten by others, and he begins to remember how *he* felt. And as he thinks in terms of himself, he consciously becomes aware that the body does house more than that which is *seen.* When awareness comes that perceives more than the body, then the athlete begins stepping over a line that separates the competitive instinct of survival with the cooperative instinct of empathy. He "feels" for the opponent. He suffers with him to a certain degree. *He too has been there.* Not just in the body, but in the mind and in the emotions. It is here that competition no longer is competition or opposition, but it is *brotherhood.* The body is no longer my enemy. He is my brother to protect, not to kill. I no longer run him back and forth mercilessly. I now begin to play *with* him. I hit the ball to him, allowing him to keep the ball in play for a longer period. I give him part of *my* life in order to help preserve his by loaning him part of my skill. I no longer need to fight to survive, but I realize the extent he is struggling to survive so I give him a "chance" to live. I, in a way, give him back his dignity, and in return gain some for myself. My selfishness is no longer a selfishness, but a consciousness of *selfness.* It is no longer my being against his body . . . but my being *and* his being. Sports is no longer a battlefield . . . man can now cooperate and help, rather than kill and destroy. I acknowledge the *Thou,* and in the acknowledgement, I acknowledge life.

If one believes in reverence for life, one cannot maintain I-It relationships during competition. The door has to be opened to other beings, and I-Thou relationships must be cultivated. It is only through this response to other living things that *humaneness* truly exists. One cannot look upon another as one would look upon an object, and exhibit any type of humane action. Humanity is accepted only through awareness of *life* that is present. It is through this recognition of *being* that the *I* can be a totality unto itself. And this reverence to being doesn't end with respect for human life. One does not destroy animal life, or life of any kind, for the fun of it . . . or for the lack of caring. A bird's life is no less sacred than a dog's life, or a human's life, when one recognizes the importance of *life,* period.

In reality, as we know it today, sport is certainly not the easiest place to love or to care for our fellow man. Stress is on *destroying*, not on helping—on *defeating,* not on creating. One plays with the thought in his mind that to play the game one must survive. Perhaps this is what led Messersmith to say: "Winning is everything . . . actually, what I want to do is *not to lose.* It's like fighting a war—you're not fighting to kill, you're fighting to stay alive." (17, p. 24) To participate, one must try to come out on top; to be anyone in sport, one must win. "He has to win. He feels that anything less will not be enough, not silver, not bronze. 'If you don't make it you are nothing,' he says." (157, p. 16)

Certainly, under these conditions, it is the *It* that receives the supreme emphasis. Can sport develop the humaneness of man? Not under our present system. The *It* overshadows the *Thou*. Win or be fired . . . be unfeeling and run up the score . . . break records at the expense of others. Sport and competition in most cases is cold and impersonal because of the goals we have cultivated in our overall society. We are taught to "be tough," to "be a killer," to "get the other guy before he gets you." Phil Woolpert made this statement: " . . . there are so many demands on your time—and, in a way, so many demands on your morality—at those high levels of competition . . . the pressure to win can corrupt—insidiously and unconsciously—the whole structure of a university. Hell, the structure of a whole society." (95, p. 78)

But even so, the dynamics of sport has the *potential* for allowing the discovery of the *Thou,* at least to a few who open themselves to it. Sport has the ingredients for allowing the individual to "find" himself. Athletics and competition offers the *place* where one can meet oneself as one is. And amid the survival instinct and the conquest desire, sport at times allows one to transcend the immediate goals and to view what *is there.* And it is there. The chance to relate with others, the chance to experience what *really* exists within our own private worlds and the world in general, the chance to touch on moments of tender humaneness . . . it is all there . . . if man could determine his priorities and seek that of importance. So within the freedom of the movement that transpires in sport, there is the freedom of choice. It is the individual who must choose whether to seek the It or the Thou. "True liberty flows, then, from our being freed from automatism. To be free is to become oneself once more, not the biological self of reflexes, of inexorable mechanisms that impede the flow of life, but the self of the person." (217, p. 218)

Usually, it seems that the best performances come in the

presence of a *Thou,* rather than in the presence of an *It.* One feels he is a vital part of what is taking place; he feels a certain amount of contact with life forces beyond his own; he seems to draw on a power greater than that he possesses in his impersonal and detached world. "We never have more strongly the impression of personal life, of self-discovery, than in that moment when we feel ourselves going beyond ourselves, carried along by a force which comes not from us, but from God." (217, p. 232)

It seems that when one turns his back on a *feeling* performance, one does not confront an experience that *moves* the individual in all of his living potential, but one is just a part of a mechanical and automatic existence. As a result, life in its wholeness and its *feeling* is ignored . . . and the individual has the sensation of having missed out on something.

One has to be objective at times. One has to deal with the It world of the self as well as the Thou world of the self . . . but to become a willing part of the *It* world and cut the ties to the emotions and the feeling world of the *Thou,* is to isolate one from contact with a *living* life. "Relation is mutual. My *Thou* affects me, as I affect it." (29, p. 15)

Experiences in sport are more than numerical scores, and statistics, and records. It is *emotion* piled on to *feeling* piled on to *sensations,* piled on to *struggle.* To recognize it as less is to lose what one could gain through a Thou participation. For through the Thou, one becomes a valid part of the *present.* One *is* at that moment and at that point in time. Sport is living in the *here and now;* one doesn't have to wait until tomorrow to affirm that one is. One *exists* in the moment one blocks a shot, or falls to the floor from a loss of balance, or when the body slices through the water in a perfectly executed dive. When the athlete is completely open to his movements, he goes *beyond* objectivity and *becomes* himself with all the many emotions and sensations present in the situation. He no longer is a distant *It* in a flowing world, but he is a close *Thou* and a vital *part* of the flow. In his openness to his actions, he *meets* his realness in a real world. "All real living is meeting." (29, p. 11)

Some athlete's movements are limited and are stereotyped. The perfect score in gymnastics comes only from the perfect move of a predetermined standard. The diver must enter the water correctly or her score suffers. Yet, one must bring his or her self into the movement or there is *nothing* there. One brings his own expression of his self by his manner of performing even though the routine as such might already be set. This is known as style; in a unique, personal way one stamps his name on his act. The high bar has the same standards for everyone, but Forsberg brought his own famous Forsberg "flop" to the bar. Certain movements are involved in the mechanics of swimming the front crawl, and yet within these movements all swimmers have their own individual styles. This is how the self and the movements combine for a relationship that is strictly personal and a *Thou* relation of the self *with* the self. One brings the being to the action.

> Spirit is not in the *I* but between *I* and *Thou.* It is not like the blood that circulates in you, but like the air in which you breathe. Man lives in the spirit, if he is able to respond to his *Thou.* He is able to, if he enters into relation with his whole being. Only in virtue of his power to enter into relation is he able to live in the spirit. (29, p. 39)

When one brings his *whole* spirit into the action, it prevents the performance from being divorced from the individual. *He* is the performance, and yet he is more than the athlete performing. He is his self, and as such he is intimately related to what he *does* as he performs. In the same way, he is intimately related to what he *feels* (about himself and others) during the performance.

So, humaneness is achieved when the athlete meets the opponent or the performance in a personal and a feeling way. He brings his life to another's life. He absorbs the being and the existence and the needs of another rather than isolating his life and ignoring the *realness* and the *presence* of those he competes against.

Since athletes go through so much themselves, they should be able to understand and to sense what others "feel." One who has felt fear in a particular situation can understand the fear of another in the same type situation. One *knows* the feeling for one has *felt* it. There is no way an athlete could describe what he actually feels when he wins a gold medal in the Olympics after years of training, but any athlete who has been through the same type training program and who has had the same goal, senses the preciousness of the moment. There is an *awareness* of feeling through empathy.

Situations in sport, whether they are based on I-You, I-It, or I-Thou relationships, are constantly changing. Every moment brings new decisions, new movements, new strategy, new feelings. The only thing that really stays constant is the man (or the I). Anything outside the sphere of man himself must be identified as such, and related to. A relationship between the individual and *things,* or between the individual and other *men,* is relevant only as experienced by the individual. Objects and things exist . . . but they become real in a man's world only when they exist in relation to the man. Until man *experiences* a fall, there is no fall. So only that which is experienced by the individual is relevant to that individual. *You* can hit a home run and experience all the emotional and physical pleasures involved in the feat . . . but that home run does not exist for me if I am unaware of it. One must open to what *is* to bring it into one's own private world. Reality may exist, but it does not exist *for me* until I am a part of it.

Simply said, I possess the *potential* for realness in the sports world, but for countless reasons I may not find it or achieve it in each sport situation. The realness is there if I can but locate it and become a part of it, and relate to it.

Man has the ingredients to find this realness. He has the power of thought and of feeling and of movement. As a result, he has the power to move *toward* the self, or away from fulfilment of the being.

Chapter 6

SPORT AND TEAM RELATIONSHIPS

Human life does not come from isolation, nor does it become nurtured by becoming an island all to itself. All life is dependent upon other life in some degree or form. The human, as it seeks significant meaning, must be aware of the importance of this relationship with other things and other beings. Probably the man who expressed this so well was Albert Schweitzer:

Affirmation of life is the spiritual act by which man ceases to live unreflectively and begins to devote himself to his life with reverence in order to raise it to its true value. To affirm life is to deepen, to make more inward, and to exalt the will to live. (246, p. 126)

In thinking about a philosophy of sport, we must be aware of an interacting of philosophical thought. One, that of individualism, is bound up in a doctrine that sees man as a being that is "personalized." The philosophy of collectivism sees man in a relationship with others within the society. Certainly, the individual is a total being within himself, yet at the same time, he must be able to relate with others to reach his own great heights as an individual.

This is something that must be kept in mind when one explores the dynamics of a *team* in the sports world. A team is composed of individuals . . . it is made up of individual athletes with individual selfhoods, even though *called* a team. It is not a *group* of athletes that makes the team, it is *individual* athletes.

The other thing the writers *always* harped on was that I wasn't a team man. This had to hurt me. But you can say anything you want about the game of baseball, it's an *individual* game first, and it's impossible for me to help you field the ball or for me to hit the ball for you. The best thing I can do for you is give encouragement. I can't do your job. (236, p. 36)

Yet, without some type of common bond, it cannot even be called a team with any amount of pride. So the problem in forming a philosophy of sport is to take into consideration the importance of the individual in relationship to the group. It is an easy thing to lose a sense of the self in athletics where demands are made on the individual for the good of the team, but a team is a true team only when the *individuals* can form a working *team relationship*.

A team consists of many individuals pooling their resources in order to gain a specific goal as a group. During this pursuit of victory or whatever the common goal might be, there are moments when the interaction of personalities is such that one or more of the individuals may be threatened as an individual during the seeking of the common goal. For instance, one serves as the "decoy" in football while the real action goes on somewhere else.

Interaction of relationships can be *mutually* beneficial in some areas of sport. In individual and duel sports, one may find that there is a give and a take that does not threaten to destroy the feeling of identity or self of either individual. In tennis doubles, for instance, the individual might set up an overhead smash for her partner by a hard-hit drive across the net. Although the credit for the putaway smash is given to the partner, both individuals are aware of the importance of the preceding shot that made the point possible. "Way to go, partner." is a common expression used following a shot of this kind.

However, sometimes in team sports, the contributions of the individual are lost in the total picture of what the *team* is doing. When individuals feel threatened, or when the self becomes subjugated to the mass, man finds it very hard to relate to that which threatens him. He either exerts his independence or he "sells his soul." Thus, the ball hog dribbles the ball to exert his identity as an individual among many, the tennis player clowns on the court, and the football player becomes a "problem" by breaking training rules and refusing to show up for practice.

117

As much as one hears about the many commendable traits taught by athletics, one must be aware of the fact that sport does not usually encourage altruism and unselfishness, as much as it develops the ability to *co-exist*. "The person becomes conscious of himself as sharing in being, as co-existing, and thus as being." (29, p. 63) One simply takes the easy way and rather than fighting the forces that threaten him, or giving in to them, one neutralizes them by isolating oneself from any binding, interacting, or *caring* relationships. One "does not care what happens"; one simply goes out and does his job. Here there are no *happenings* for one is not open to such forces.

Because of the importance of the *self* to the individual, no one gives up his rights willingly, not even in the sports world. Nor should one ask a man to sacrifice at the expense of himself in the sports world any more than one should in the business world, or in any other facet of life. Yet, if the purpose is team victory, there are situations where sacrifice is the only way. The batter "sacrifices" in baseball to advance the runner. The track player becomes the "rabbit" to help a teammate win the race. The fullback "fakes" into the line to allow the halfback to sweep the end. But there is a difference between a temporary sacrifice, and the more permanent one of *life forces.* One gets over a temporary sacrifice such as advancing the runner. One never gets over sacrificing the *self.* Perhaps it is this basic fear that the *total* being is being sacrificed that prevents many players from belonging to a team, or being a team player even to a limited extent. As Bill Russell puts it: " . . . too many coaches view their prospective athletes as performers and not as people." (187, p. 82)

Then too, the whole philosophy of sport as our culture sees it is team *against* team, individual *against* individual. The whole concept of our sports' oriented culture is that of *opposition,* not of cooperation. We go out to *beat* the opponent, to *defeat* the other team, to *conquer* on the athletic field.

Here the important thing is not the goal but the relationship to the "others"; not one's own victory but the others' failure. In this new-style competition people are often in doubt whether there is a race at all, and if so, what its goals are. Since they are supposed to be cooperative rather than rivalrous, they may well feel guilt about success. (179, pp. 104-105)

We never, or very rarely, think in terms of going out to play *with* the other team in order that *we* might each gain something of pleasure and of value. So it is a small wonder that the athletic field becomes a place of survival for the fittest for most athletes, where the key to the game is to survive longer than the opponent . . . which means winning at any cost.

One thinks nothing of using objects to help one advance in sports. One uses the bat to hit the ball; one utilizes the pole to clear the high bar; one uses the football to pass for a first down, or the basketball to pass down court for the fast break. The objects are non-living, and therefore, they are subject to the desires of man. Yet, even the athlete is used by others, not only by the opponent but even by his teammates. The basketball player uses a teammate as a screen in order to get off the shot. The football player goes into the game for one play to act as a messenger for the coach. The gymnast uses another to "spot" for her, and as mentioned before, the "rabbit" in track runs to set the pace for *another*.

In speaking of the "rabbit" in tract, Howard Slusher says:

Not only does man no longer run with man, nor even against man, now he runs against an artificial standard *using* man to assist his efforts. Is this not the height of human decay? Man *uses* another. And perhaps what is worse, man allows and offers himself to be used . . . it is not enough for man to run for the sake of running or even for victory. Man now becomes the *tool* and even the slave instrument of measurement. Man is not important. Records are important." (202, p. 175)

However, this author does not agree with Slusher that the use of another person to obtain a goal is "human decay." Man has always attempted to help his fellow man, and men have always allowed themselves to be "used" when they deemed the end result important enough. As long as a man *willingly* gives himself, and as long as another does not use this gift *selfishly,* then it must be classified as cooperation . . . not as slave labor. The difference is whether one is *forced* into being used, or *volunteers* to be used.

However, when the primary object of sport is to win, many times the "good of the team" takes prerequisite over individual rights, and man is then *forced* into sacrificing parts of himself if he wishes to be a part of the team. Even then, it becomes a matter of choice as one chooses the higher value of *teamwork.* When one wishes to win over and above everything else, all along the road man finds himself negating a little more and a little more of himself, until there is nothing left of a *single* victory, located solely in the dignity of the individual.

One can hold onto this potential of the self only by realizing that the relation one has to one's self and the relation one has to a teammate or the team is *not the same.* The responsibility to the *I* precedes the responsibility to the team when the concept of the *I* is a *true* one . . . and is built on a feeling of *selfness,* not *selfishness.*

In many instances, the use of others comes about as a result of the framework of sport. Man is pressured into giving up many of his freedoms in athletics because he is continually pushed into doing what is good for the *team.* He sacrifices his own individual style in order to fit into the *team* style. He gives up his freedom of thought in order to do what he has been *told* to do by the coach. He is not asked to be an *individual*, but a *team member.* And it could be no other way if our concepts of a team and of teamwork were to have any type of basis.

The thing that we so often miss in the overall picture is that even though a team is opposing another team, it is made up of individuals. The team does not necessarily make a fast break, but the individual player does so by the initial pass out from beneath the defensive basket. The team does not hit the spike, the individual does, although the set-up by a teammate made it possible (and even here the team did not make the set-up, the individual did). A team is never truly a team, even though the individual players may perform in such a unified manner that one thinks in terms of *the team.* The players have simply been put together in such a disciplined manner that they "fit" to-

120

gether as they pursue a common goal. "The only way all our peculiar, strong personalities could be coordinated into one great team was to constantly work toward the one single goal." (187, p. 88)

On a team like this, each player wants to win worse than he wants to be a "star," therefore, he individually cooperates with teammates to obtain this end. But even when unified as such for a common purpose, there is a certain line drawn by players which they will not cross even for the team. Many gripes on teams come about when this line has been approached, or when they have been *forced* to cross it, thereby losing some of their individuality that is important to their concept of *self*. "I've always criticized myself for the times I've let other guys dictate what happened to me. Like going someplace I didn't want to go or eating late." (235, p. 32)

This concept of self is illustrated in the fact that a player will go in willingly in the last five seconds of a close basketball game; however, the same player might be insulted to be sent in for the last five seconds of a "run-away" game. In the tight game, he is being sent in for a specific purpose. The coach in some way feels he is the person who can make the difference in the team's play in those last five seconds that might result in a victory. He is being used as a *potential*. His self is important because even though working for a team victory, he is a *necessary* and needed part. Vallely, while playing at UCLA, recognized this difference when he said:

> When Ecker won that game for us, it gave us a special lift because he was a substitute who did it. It meant he contributed something that none of the starters could. It was better that way. I rememer last year's championship, and a lot of guys didn't feel anything about it because they didn't think they had contributed. (102, p. 11)

However, to be sent in for the last five seconds of a game where there is twenty or thirty points difference is simply a *token* substitution. The coach is substituting the individual just to get everybody in the game, and so the player can say he played in the game. But the player knows he has not *played* in

121

the game for five seconds. Five seconds does not allow him the potential to *affect* the play or the results. His presence is a *nothing*, for not only can he have no affect on the final results, but he also has no real chance for a vital participation in five seconds if the objective has been victory all along. His *self* has no real purpose in that game for those five seconds, and he feels insulted that he has been *used* in this way.

It is hard to keep individual freedom and individuality in the sports world. Everyone wants a clean cut hair style . . . the team must dress as a team . . . there is always pressure for the athlete to maintain a good "public image," etc. There is a constant struggle to keep some kind of peace with the self while being grabbed at and pulled at by *team* desires and needs. Jack Scott must have felt some of these pressures when he made the following comment:

> I believe for a human being to be contented, he has to express his uniqueness. When a person is young, he has not yet developed the cognitive skills. Physical activity is one of the most natural ways of self-expression. But a kid goes to college, and he has to go through his paces like an animal. He has no control or say in the program, in deciding who he will compete against and what will be the nature of the competition. (195, pp. 45-46)

One tries to hold unto the self while maintaining rapport with the team. One must decide what part of the self can be given up without killing that which one might be seeking. Man looks for peace within himself while participating in an activity that fosters violence and battle, and there is a continual paradox in *searching for* and *giving away*.

There are some things that man must keep for the self if he is to maintain a working relationship with his own individualism. He can't be a clog in a machine and be a creative and unique individual at the same time. He must hang onto what is important to him without allowing others to make him feel guilty for what he is and for what he enjoys doing . . . for his possibility *to be* is tied up in his enjoyment of what he is. Even today, with all the hero worship of athletes, the individual who

Courtesy of Brevard College. Bill Boggs, Photographer.

takes part in athletics is often looked down on by the intellectual segment of our society. This negativism, especially toward women's sports, leaves the athlete with a sense of guilt that he or she is an athlete. By feeling guilty because of the value given to the opinions of others, the woman athlete, in many cases, has given away her freedom to be herself in space and time conducive to her own personal development. She loses some of her own reality because she denies herself the joy and pride in *being* what she is. She denies herself the full pleasure in her movement, her coordination, her *personal experiencing* of physical and mental action.

But while holding unto the self and its joy in *being,* the athlete must be careful that he or she doesn't take another man's or woman's freedom for his or her own gain. He must allow other men their opportunities to be and to become, just as he would protect his own for his own selfhood. He will find his own reality in the involvement, if he can hold himself open to the experience, and not give away too much of his self for external goals based on *group* decisions.

Even while most individuals cannot give themselves *completely* to the team, teamwork still does exist, but not in the sense we usually give it. Teamwork is an outcropping of overlapping goals, not from the fusion of individuals into a *oneness.* The individual remains just that . . . an individual . . . even when the group's achievement might suggest that the individual has been swallowed up in collectivism. He has not been "swallowed up." He has simply been directing his identity into the same channels that others have chosen.

And although statistics and scores given are those indicating team performance, actually what has happened has been that many *individual* performances have been geared toward a common objective. Even though the *team* may have played poorly, an individual may have had a great night, and even though the team may be getting beat, the individual may still be winning an individual battle with an individual opponent. Consequently, a player plays *with* the team—or more truthfully—a player plays *with other* individuals on the team. One does not lose one's identity when one plays *with* a team. One may easily lose one's identity when one plays only *for* a team.

When one plays *with* a team, one offers to share oneself with others while maintaining the right to *individual being.* This sharing lends itself to what is called team unity, but it does not mean the individual is allowing his being to be *blended* into the mass at the expense of his own individuality. But the fact that *an* individual is willing to play with the team doesn't give the team real substance as a team. For a team to give the impression of, and *to be,* what we signify when we say "team," *all* of the individual members must be working toward the same objective rather than pursuing different individual ends.

When the team goal is the same as the goal chosen by the individuals making up the team, then the individuals are no longer playing only *with* the team, but also *for* the team . . . or more specifically, *for the team objective.* Even so, the individuals remain separate in their *being,* giving unification to the group by their willingness to *share* of themselves for the group purpose, but not to *give* themselves to another or to the group (for where individual being is important, there is always the holding back of the *total self.* This self belongs to the individual, not to a group of individuals).

Man keeps his being while *relating* with others, not by attempting to *become another. He* is within the framework. *Teamness* comes through means of a single objective, rather than by the development of *one being* at the loss of several *individual beings.* There is a *unification* of individuality which results in teamness—but not a *sacrifice* of individuality.

This unification or striving toward a common goal is what we should build our concept of team spirit on; otherwise, we tend to separate man from the reality of his individual being. Man is a contributing factor to the good of the whole only when he can maintain his *own* wholeness. He does this through free choice, picking the values that are pertinent to his own life force as well as to the life force of the team. He stands independent *within* himself, while the team stands dependent *upon* him as an individual. Realizing the relationship, he also realizes the responsibility. He plays as a free man, but because he is free, he allows himself to *choose* to be a contributing factor to the team goal. One does not become subordinated when one becomes a member of a team, but one becomes responsible for oneself *and* for others. But it is not forced. This responsibility is accepted willingly. He *is* playing, but he is playing *with* others. "A person makes his appearance by entering into relation with other persons." (29, p. 62)

Man is not motivated to *feel* by external forces, but feels because of what he is inside. Therefore, team spirit and team rapport cannot be externally motivated by the coach, but comes about as a result of the internal feelings of *each* individual on the team toward one another. To ask a player to do something for the sake of the team without regard for his rights as an individual, is to force him into a corner where he must deny himself as an entity, and subjugate himself to the total "thing" that denies him his individuality. This type of external pressure makes man into something he is not, and leads him to contribute to a thing of lesser importance than his being. *However,* if the player sincerely and actually cares about the others around him because of what he *is* as an individual, his contribution toward the welfare of the team will come voluntarily as a *giving* to those around him because of the realization of the importance of the beings relating to each other on the team. This is when "team spirit" really exists . . . when individuals feel a reverence or a responsibility to the life forces of others because of the reality of the life force of the self. According to Vince Lombardi:

What I missed most was—well, it *wasn't* the tension and the crowds and the game on Sunday. And it certainly *wasn't* the winning. And it *wasn't* the spotlight and all that. The fame. No, it wasn't. There's a great—a great *closeness* on a football team, you know—a rapport between the men and the coach that's like no other sport. It's a binding together, a knitting together." (93, p. 33)

When team members can relate to each other, there is not isolation between the self and others. " . . . what creates in me consciousness of being a person is entering into relationship with another person, the 'thou.' " (217, p. 125) Identity of the self is never completely separate from that which evolves around it. The individual is a part of his commitment, and as such is a part of the total life. Consequently, *the* team becomes *my* team, and in the full moment of relation, it becomes *our* team. *We* win, or *we* played, even though what has actually taken place is that *many individuals* have contributed in their own unique way toward a common interest. " . . . one of the most beautiful things to see is a group of men coordinating their efforts toward a common goal—alternately subordinating and asserting themselves to achieve real teamwork in action." (186, p. 18) The team as such is not *I,* but *we;* yet, without the I, there can be no we.

But the player must not lose his sense of the *I* in preference to *group* being. A group has importance only in relationship to the importance of the *individuals* making up the group. One might say that when a team has spirit, it is because the individual finds identity with the other individuals on the team, rather than identity with the mass known as *the* team.

In team sports, the big problem is how one gets the maxi-

126

mum potential from each indivual in order to attain a goal as a team. There must be a common denominator that each individual is working for if a "team spirit" is to prevail. Every individual must be interested in the same basic results, or else the team loses its unification. A volleyball team may present a picture of so many unorganized parts during pre-season practice, and yet when the actual competition starts, they "jell" into a team. Why? Possibly during the pre-season practice, each individual is looking out for his basic interest—making the team. Then when these basic interests have been met in one way or another (she makes it or she doesn't), during the regular season, she is free to channel her interests toward a different goal . . . that of winning . . . and this is impossible without a working relationship between the other individuals on the team.

If winning, or a common goal is not basic to each individual during the season, then the team may never "jell" into a team, but will continue to be a group of individuals seeking individualized interests. The coach usually serves as a catalyst in moulding a team into a group of *one* in a sense. Jerry Kramer spoke of Vince Lombardi in this way: "He made us hate him much of the time, but even this hatred, this half-serious suspicion that he treated us like dogs, served to unify us. We had a single target for all our frustrations . . . " (106, p. 52)

However, it should be remembered that the team is composed of separate individuals with unique personalities and a *personal* sense of responsibility to the self. Along with this sense of responsibility to self, the coach must cultivate a responsibility to the group. This is not an easy thing, for to accomplish this, it means that individuals must avocate some of their individual freedom in order to fulfil the purpose of the group. This giving up of individual freedom does not necessarily mean that an individual changes his being as much as it means he lets his life forces be *channeled* into certain types of behavior patterns in order to work within the framework of what is expected of the *mass* of players. But even this willingness to let others choose what form his life will take in order to have a *real* team means quite a sacrifice to the individual who cherishes his free choice and his individual independence. Many individuals are unable to make this sacrifice. One reads of many of the "problem" ath-

127

letes. In many cases, it conceivably grows out of the inability of the athlete to subjugate his individuality to that of the team.

Sometimes, when certain types of individuals make up a team, the team itself becomes correlated with these particular individuals. For instance, the Chicago Bears are "rough," the Green Bay Packers are a "power" team, etc. In a way, this symbolic characteristic of the team as a result of a *few* members generally results in *all* the team members having these characteristics as they try to "measure up" to their reputation. Although it may not be noticeable to the general public, oftentimes, there are teams within the team. This occurs when individuals become even more united because of their relationship to each other, than because of their relationship to the total group. Some of the best known groups are interior linemen in football. For instance, the "Fearsome Foursome."

But even though some teams pick up a reputation for characteristics of individual players, a team is not dependent on the separate identities of the players. It has a form of its own. Even if the star player is hurt, and must sit out a game, the *team* still plays.

Individual athletes are *part* of the team, and as such must give up certain individual rights in order to play *for* the team. Emphasis is not on individual dignity, but on team dignity. Some players *are* used as decoys and as "rabbits." Others are simply *there,* as they sit on the bench and watch the game since they are *substitutes.* One might ask: substitutes for what? For the real thing? For the real players? For the team? In a sense, they cannot substitute *for* the team, but must substitute for a specific individual. Yet, they too are only a clog in the whole, so that when they enter the game, they too go in to play *for* the team, not for the individual they substituted for. If a *true* team exists, individual desires and goals are sacrificed for the good of the team. There is no other way, for anything less than this makes it less than a team, and the individual athletes are relagated to being individuals, and not a team. In order to maintain this "teamness," the individuals must maintain some type of rapport with each other . . . this is done through communication, either on an artificial level done consciously to maintain workable relations within the team, or on a subconscious level

128

where the indivuals *actually care* for each other as members of the same team. As expressed by Lew Alcindor: "When we finished the year with our third straight NCAA championship, I somehow wasn't as impressed by the victory as I was by the way a group of very different men had come together in tolerance and affection." (4, p. 43)

Many coaches speak of the unity their teams have, of the feeling of brotherhood their players have. Jerry Kramer said: "There's a great deal of love for one another on this club. Perhaps we're living in Camelot." (107, p. 217) It is true that the intenseness of the sport situation can lead to a sharing of relationships, which in some cases comes close to our definition of love for others.

However, because of human nature, it cannot be said that *all* sports situations lead to brotherhood or to sharing or to caring, or even to loving. Bill Bradley tried to describe this: "On every sports team there are conflicts. Pro teams are made of conflicts. It is their nature; we are all competing. Why we succeed and why it is such a pleasure to be here is because . . . our conflicts never turn to bitterness." (46, p. 16) It is against human nature to sacrifice the self for the good of the majority. It is against normal drives to be willing to give up individual freedom and dignity for the "good of the team." Competition does not promote altruism; if anything, it reinforces just the opposite. Man in most instances competes *to win*, not to lose—and especially to win his individual selfhood, *not to lose* his being among the masses. As a result, teammates are not always friends. They do not *always* really care about each other. " . . . I truly believe that teammates cannot be friends. It would be too much of a strain. The most that teammates can be is what I call 'strong acquaintances.' " (187, p. 88) But there are a few rare occasions when one *does* love teammates . . . when one *does* care about others one competes with and against. The possibility is there . . . and when one finds it, one tries to protect it by being responsible to the value of it.

So what do we mean when we speak of teamwork? Probably the only way to describe the dynamics of teamwork is to say that man *cooperates* in order to achieve the goals of the team, but in doing so, he allows himself to keep his self intact by cooperating in order to achieve as a *person. He* is the one that jumps, and shoots, and runs . . . not the team. *He* is the one that improves daily through practice, and as a result, makes the team better. *He* is the one that scores the goal and makes the points although the credit is given to the team. So it is through the opportunity to develop and to achieve as a person, *along* with the team, that the individual cooperates in order to be a part of the team.

Courtesy of Clear Creek High School. John Burr, Photographer.

The team cannot *force* the individual to cooperate unless he is willing to do so, for if he is coerced through rules and outward restrictions imposed by the team beyond the willingness to *give* up of his self *to* the team, he simply quits the team and is no longer a part. We see this happening more and more today. Athletes who feel they are being *exploited as individuals* are taking their gripes to the highest levels, and in many instances are picketing for the firing of the coach. These gripes range from racism to the cutting of long hair. One baseball player took his case to court ["Flood is contending baseball's reserve clause, which binds a player to one club until he is traded or released, results in a player being treated like a piece of property and is in violation of antitrust laws." (78, p. 14)] and many others are testing their rights through legal channels.

Individuals in our world today are more conscious of individuality than at any other period of time.

> University deans, trustees, Presidents of the United States, generals, policemen, parents, the Pope—nearly every symbol of authority—had a very rough time during the '60s . . . Baseball players defied owners who wanted to trade them; black athletes rebelled against coaches who wanted to run their lives. Two new sins—"unresponsiveness" and "irrelevance"—were discovered during the '60s and found to lurk around almost every seat of power and, some said, within the democratic system itself. (215, pp. 14-15)

Even in athletics, where the power of the coach and the good of the team were absolutes never questioned, individuals are beginning to make their selves felt. Some have quit to join hippie colonies, while others have turned to publications to make their gripes known. "Chip" Oliver explained why he quit pro football to become a hippie in this way: "Football dehumanizes people. They've taken the players and made them into slabs of beef that can charge around and hit each other." (169, p. 21) In a world overly sensitive to individual rights, sport has been one of the last strongholds . . . but in the coming years, it will have its share of problems since the team is no longer the thing of primary importance . . . it is every man for *himself.*

Does this mean that "team spirit" and "teamwork" is a thing of the past? No. But its accomplishment can no longer be *forced* without being *questioned* by individuals. One cannot *make* the individual work for the good of the team through outward means. The individual works for the team because he *wants* to, and is motivated *within* rather than from without. A man *allows* himself to act as a decoy and to be sacrificed and to be substituted at the whims of the coach because he *wants* to be a part of the team. And if he does desire to take part under the conditions of having to give up a part of himself "for the good of the team," he usually does so because he does not fear *losing* himself, but is aware of the chance to *find* himself through personal achievement as a participant.

This willingness to give up some things in order to have the chance to gain other things is what makes man willing to be part of a "thing" that has a certain amount of control over his being. As a result of this cooperation, a feeling of teamwork does evolve and does exist. "I used to think a lot and talk a lot about what I called the love on our team, the feeling that each Packer had for all his teammates, and sometimes I wondered whether this spirit produced victory or whether victory produced this spirit." (106, p. 55) There is a feeling of "togetherness" because *all* of the individuals "are in the same boat," so to speak. Each is searching for an identity *through* the team, and as such, each must accept the other's validity as a part of the team.

For a team to succeed, there must be a feeling of responsibility on the part of each individual. One is *responsible* for what one contributes, as well as for what one does *not* contribute. One is also responsible for helping *others* on the team to contribute toward the team goal. Sometimes, one helps the team to succeed because of selfish reasons. For instance, one knows that if the team wins, the individual also profits in many ways. Yet, working toward a goal, whether for selfish purposes or not, is a form of being responsible. One is showing responsibility toward the well-being of oneself. Responsibility as a team member in the sports world does not grow out of the necessity to survive or to exist, as much as it grows out of the necessity to *succeed.* Teamwork is based on responsibility. Every member must share in the responsibility if the team is to have the *shape* of actually being a team. This form or shape of the team comes from the totality of individual purposes, which results only from a sense of responsibility to a specific value. As the players work toward a common goal, and respond in a responsible way in order to attain this goal, the individuals seem to *fit;* consequently, the team looks organized and plays *like* a team. Being responsible for exerting effort which will aid the cause, team members *relate* to each other, and individual meaning gives meaning which is seen as *the team,* rather than as many separate individuals. However, total *team* objectives may not be equal to the sum of all the separate individual objectives, since one often has to sacrifice *personal* desires to help the team win. When all the players are willing to work toward a common goal (even at the expense of individuality at times), then the form of the team becomes apparent as we say the players are beginning to "shape up." Other common expressions are "if we can just *jell* together we will have a fine team," or "everything is beginning to *click together* now."

If the team is to succeed, each individual must share in the responsibility necessary to make it succeed. This includes following training rules, utilizing skills for the "good of the team," giving "100 per cent," etc. Another way one shows responsibility is in decision making. When everyone on the team agrees with a specific decision, it carries the connotation of a "team decision." Actually, the decision has been an *individual* decision, since the team as such does not have an existence outside of the individuals making up the team. At the same time, even though a majority of players might make a decision a "team" decision, if it is opposed by one or several of the team members, it is not in reality a team decision, but actually represents what the *majority* of the team feels. So there is really no such thing as a team decision. There are individual decisions made by team members, but when all members have mutual interests and are geared toward the same goal, then one speaks of them as a team . . . even though in actuality, they are a group of individuals seeking the same end. At times, this factor probably leads to play that is unpredictable as individual members of the team seek goals that are more in line with their own individual interests. One of the big jobs of coaching is channeling the individual interests toward a *single* goal so that teamwork is the result.

However, there is more to team responsibility than that only geared toward success. Responsibility includes a sense of responsibility for the vital forces of others. It includes caring for the welfare of other individuals along with the welfare of the self. This type of responsibility is taken on voluntarily, and no amount of "team" pressure can create this *feeling* for others.

One cannot *force* the athlete into willingly taking on humaneness if his real being is opposed to the responsibility. As Howard Slusher says: " ... a *true* construct of responsibility would demonstrate the athlete to be one who not only plays within the rules, but *responds* within the rules to another in such a way that it exhibits real reflection and concern with others' needs." (202, p. 77)

In situations where teammates *do* relate to one another, and where there is real caring and sharing, the *I* allows for the existence of the *Thou,* and there is responsibility for both self and others. Roosevelt Grier expressed it this way: "You see, that's the whole thing about a football team or an entertainment team, you got to help the other guy up or the whole thing goes down. And the higher you pull him up, the higher *you* go." (56, p. 67) Therefore, a type of *dualism* exists without either the I or the Thou threatening one or the other. On the other hand, the I and Thou *reinforce* the importance of each other's existence. "Lots of joy out there on that field, lot of love. But the big thing you learn: *You always need ten other guys."* (56, p. 67)

But within all the violence and all the struggle, and as the individual in a sense fights to live, to remain in the game—it is rare instances when *real* love exists between the players. Many never reach this feeling of caring for the opponent, or for their teammates, because the conflict present in competition does not encourage one to be his "brother's keeper," as much as it encourages him to be his "brother's conqueror," When one seeks to control and to rule over another, one seldom develops an environment of love in the process. Some do, however, for I have witnessed it in a few rare, precious moments. The struggle almost drowns out any close relationships, but the *potential* is there, and sometimes the fierce competition *does* give way to kindness, and one does come face to face with values beyond winning.

I was misty-eyed myself I felt so good. I felt so proud, proud of myself and proud of my teammates and proud of my coaches. I felt like I was a part of something special. I guess it's the way a group of scientists feel when they make a big breakthrough ... It's a feeling of being together, completely together, a singleness of purpose, accomplishing something that is very difficult to accomplish, accomplishing something that a lot of people thought you couldn't accomplish. It sent a beautiful shiver up my back." (107, p. 199)

It is these rare moments of feeling *together* that brings such *intenseness* to living, for if one can experience an emotion like love, or even caring, in the midst of the violent struggle for victory, then there must be hope that men may still learn to live with one another through recognition of the value of life in *any* situation.

One of the great things about sport is that opponents *may* evolve from an *It* object one is trying to defeat, to a *Thou* that one respects and cares for *in spite* of the fight for a common goal. It is true, however, that few athletes get anything more out of competition than competition. *Reverence for others* is an unknown feeling for the majority of players ... they go to conquer, and this they do ... but they miss out on the glory. One becomes, and is, many times, without *knowing* the other. But for the individual to confront reality in its wholeness, he must be able to relate—not as *I* and *It,* but as *I* and Thou. Without the reverence and the respect, there is no *real* relationship. "Through the *Thou* a man becomes *I.*" (29, p. 28)

This sense of relating can come from the *We* relationship on a team, but even in the *We,* there is a separation. The individual stands apart from the full reverence of the Thou, and yet is a part of the total. There is no *oneness* in the "we." There is you and me and others. This is at least a start in the possibility that someday I might recognize you as the *Thou.*

Some teams find everything at once ... the winning and the caring, such as the Green Bay Packers while being coached by Vince Lombardi. The better teams seem to have this feeling of "love" toward each other. When much is *shared* together, much seems to be *felt* together. Teams win and lose, laugh and cry, hope and despair ... all *together* as a team. As they play *with* each other, they feel *for* each other. This willingness to share

135

and to care for others allows the athlete to explore the wholeness of his own individual life. He opens himself up to boundaries beyond himself that *includes others*. He becomes a part of a total human existence rather than an isolated single human life. Consequently, he allows a maximum development by not cutting himself off from that which would make him more than what he is. He allows himself to be *bonded* to other life voluntarily through his caring and his empathy ... as a result, he accepts responsibility for that beyond himself, and existence takes on added meaning. He is no longer an *I*, but an I that cares for the *Thou*.

If sport is to have any *lasting* meaning, each participant must care. Whether we want it or not, it is "our" season, and "our" team. And whether we recognize it or not, the team is more meaningful when I have a sense of responsibility that makes it "my" team. One must identify with what one is a part of.

Spectators sense this need for identification, as they *feel* with the team even while remaining separated from the *true* action. They are a part of it, and they are not, but by supporting the team, one reaffirms that one *cares*. Real caring, however, comes from an involvement with the action, or with the individuals caught up in the action. Caring does not develop only from the *results* of the action as seen by the many fans who only support a winner. These fans only care for the end result, but not for the vital forces that are committed to the action.

> If one does not identify with the winner but is at the very same time preoccupied with the process of winning itself ... one is prepared for the role of consumer of others' winnings ... The content of the identification is impoverished to the point where virtually the only bond between reader and hero is the fact of the hero's winning. The spectator ... wants to become involved with the winner simply in order to make the contest meaningful: this hope of victory makes the event exciting, while the game or contest or story is not appreciated for its own sake. (179, p. 107)

Spectators who are only loyal while their team is winning

care in a *superficial* way. Fans who *really* care, care *all* the time. They are *constantly* supporting their team. Perhaps this is why there was such bedlam when the Mets won the 1969 World Series. The fans had been with them from the period of ineptness to the period of greatness, and they could appreciate what many called a miracle . . . but which was a progression of growth nurtured by the *care* of many.

So many things are involved in team relationships and spectator appeal. Some go to win; some go to play; some go because they care. Without the *caring,* one misses out on the potential to be *completely involved* . . . and *bonded* to life.

Chapter 7

ANXIETY, SUFFERING, AND RISK IN ATHLETICS

There is more to sport than just recognizing that one *is* during participation. Sport also offers a place of safety, or it can offer a place of risk . . . whichever the individual is seeking to fulfil his being.

Sport offers safety, or a sense of security, by being a place where one can escape when the crowds and the pressure of a mechanized society become too much. There is a sense of safety in the order of sport, brought about by the rules which are defined so precisely.

At the same time, if an individual desires aloneness, he can choose the type of sport that will give him isolation from others.

> . . . I had always been somewhat of a loner. The self-discipline one imposed on oneself did not exactly make one the life and soul of a party. It was impossible to share your feelings with someone who did not understand the very nature of your sport. Friendship, too, probably required an amount of giving, and this I was not prepared to do. All the giving I was prepared to make was concentrated in the one area—toward making me a champion. (49, p. 21)

Anxiety and Suffering

The cross country runner, the surfer, the fisherman, the golfer, and the hunter all have a certain amount of privacy as they pursue their sport. Yet, others may choose to put their daring on the line in a sport taking place before thousands of spectators. Yet, even then, the athlete may be very much *alone* in his involvement. Regardless of the sport one engages in, the

138

athlete does not seek protection and safety even though the sport may be a "lonely" one, but he seeks self fulfilment on a very personal and intimate basis . . . if he is *truly* committed to the action he is involved in. As a result of his involvement, he becomes an individual contained within a sport—caught up in his perception of space, time, and control of body and external objects.

Courtesy of Brevard College.

This person seeking fulfilment always seems to be at the door of eternal being through his ability to be *absorbed* in his present being. He *is* at that point in time, and as such, he can not conceive of himself as *not being.* He is not an object floating in time and manipulated by fate . . . he exists as a human being, and as such, exerts his rights to life. And just as he does not expect himself to be used by the world he exists in, he does not desire to *use* sports. He is simply a part of that which he lives in. He is a part of life and a part of sport. There can only be dignity in *accepting the experience as a part of his wholeness.* He is committed to the complete action and to his being regardless of the suffering, and risk, and pain involved . . . for these things are necessary for the fulfilment. "If there is a meaning in life at all, then there must be a meaning in suffering. Suffering is an ineradicable part of life, even as fate and death. Without suffering and death human life cannot be complete." (61, p. 106)

The athlete usually finds out early that suffering is a part of the process of competing. It is the price he pays for achievement in a physical world where conditioning is attained only through hard work and principles of overload. "You have to pay the price" is a well used quote.

In practice, in the game or meet, and even afterwards, the athlete must tolerate anguish and personal suffering. According to David Smith, "When it starts to hurt, when your shoulders and legs begin turning to lead, you gotta step outside yourself. The pain is in your body, not your head." (97, p. 58) The player cannot quit because of pain without losing the meaning he has pursued. At times, the only thing that keeps him going is the fact that his torture is limited to so many minutes, or so many rounds, or so many quarters. Anyone who has even been aware of the various dynamics of life knows that suffering and tragedy are a very vital part of life . . . there is certainly no reason why sport should be exempt from it . . . if anything the degree of suffering *should* be greater in sport because of the *intenseness* of living during the sport experience.

Suffering is a relative thing when viewed in terms of what one has accomplished while enduring the pain. Some suffer more *because they wish to gain more.* Some endure little pain, for what they seek is not worth the suffering. When one is aware of the meaning of the self, pain and suffering are things one *knows* in the process of becoming. One knows them on a very intimate and personal basis. It is *mine* to bear. It is *mine to feel* in my guts. It is *mine to endure* in order to obtain a dignity of self. But for those who experience no *real* meaning within their lives, suffering also has no meaning, and becomes a burden rather than a *way* to find the goal.

Pain makes one more aware of the self. One feels many things in an intensified way when one is in pain. One becomes more aware of an ankle after it has been sprained. As a result of the

140

sprain, the ankle seems to be a very vital part of the body and the whole self is aware of the member *because* of the pain. When one hurts, one knows the part that hurts *is there*.

Courtesy of Brevard College. Bill Boggs, Photographer.

To perceive the self fully through the sports medium, one must be willing to take the pain, to risk the self, to accept danger, and to be open to a gamble. One takes a chance that one won't get hurt, that one won't suffer too badly, that one won't be "killed" by a lopsided score. All of these things are present in the life of the athlete, and leads to worry since the athlete's ability to play depends on his ability to remain healthy, or to at least live with the pain. In the words of Brian Job, "There's always a fear. You know you're not going to die, but you know that if you swim a fast time it will hurt so much, and you're afraid of that." (18, p. 29)

The makeup of sport, with its violence and warlike spirit, gives the athlete the chance to learn to live with pain, fear, and anxiety. "Survival is the name of the game," as some would

141

say—the athlete must *protect* his territory, he must *defend* his goal, he must *defeat* his opponent. He doesn't just live with fear, but he *confronts* it daily. He knows it is there . . . so by entering into the activity where it exists, he actually goes out voluntarily to meet it. He not only goes out to beat the opponent, but he goes out *to conquer fear also.* Or if he can't conquer his fear completely, he at least tries to live with it without allowing it to defeat *him.* Jim Ryan expressed it this way: "I am afraid of losing. But I can't think back to the day when I wasn't scared. It's when that fear of losing becomes so overwhelming—then it's time to quit." (141, p. 19)

Anxiety might be described as a conflict of the inner person as the individual tries to find what his potential is, and to re-affirm in a positive way *who* he is. Fear, or the feelings of not competing well, is something that is very personal. No other man can really enter into another man's fear. Each individual has his own moments he must face on an intimate basis *alone.* One usually fears what is in the future . . . the event coming up, the match *tomorrow.* This is why one loses the feelings of fear once the action starts, for it is a matter of the *now* during the actual event.

"Butterflies," or anxiety, leaves almost immediately once the game has started. One can suffer all kinds of torment—sweaty hands, heavy heartbeats . . . even upset stomach—as one waits before the game. But once the action starts, the signs of fear disappear, and one is no longer afraid. One is *within* that which one fears, and is surviving it. However, if one isn't playing as well as one thinks one should, the feelings of anxiety may come back. One begins to "tighten up," to "push harder." When the pressure becomes too great because one is not reaching his potential, one either must re-evaluate his goals or get out of sport. Perhaps this is one of the reasons why Jim Ryan quit running while still in his "running prime."

One seldom has time to fear while one is in an emergency. When one is *really* involved, one has no time to harbor imaginary failure, or doubts. One *is* coping at that moment; therefore, one does not fear for the self in the present. It is always the future one fears for. The athlete is afraid it might not be *there* that day and that time, so he becomes afraid of the

142

nothingness that might engulf him. Potentials in our culture are usually measured in terms of wins and losses. Therefore, the athlete *anticipates* he may lose and correlates this with weakness; consequently, he is afraid and nervous before he has proven himself in the game. His ability to prove himself is always a thing he waits for. He doesn't know *yet* how he will do in the match or the game. As he waits to prove himself, he does not *know* if he will win or lose—therefore, he does not *know* if he will be strong or weak during the testing period.

The athlete is afraid of future moments, when what he fears may become real rather than imagined. When the game, or the future event, is finally begun, he becomes involved in *being* and the anxiety is decreased until *another* tomorrow and *another* anticipated defeat. He correlates defeat with *not* being—or nothingness. One fears to be what one is . . . especially if one is a loser. Our society does not take kindly to losers.

Anxiety often results from a lack of meaning outside of the value of winning. When one loses, one has lost *everything,* if this is all one has sought. When meaning no longer exists for the individual, then one begins to lose the feeling of selfhood. One unconsciously *dislikes* oneself. There is a sense of uneasiness even when one is involved, whether in performing or in coaching, for what one is involved in no longer *matters.* One participates in appearance, but one is not involved in fact.

One of the most important aspects of meaning in sport is the involvement that relates to the complexity and kind of structural demands. "Sport" may even be defined as involvement; to choose to enter and re-enter the structured reality of sport is to be involved in it—to "care" about it. (59, p. 44)

If one seeks achievement on a meaningful, *personal* level rather than seeking victory only, then anxiety and fear does not have the intenseness one finds when victory is the *only* thing that counts. One can control meaning on a personal and an intimate basis . . . one cannot always control whether one wins or loses. If one gives affirmation to winning as a way of life, then there is continuous tension as one attempts to continually win. If one gives affirmation to the self, one also experiences a certain amount of tension as one seeks the self continually . . . but with it there is a certain amount of freedom and a chance to find the self during the competitive process. "Through his power to survey his life, man can transcend the immediate events which determine him." (123, p. 141)

When one is seeking affirmation of the self during competition, there is a strange happiness in the process of playing. One feels unrestrained, unhampered . . . as though one is free from bonds and can almost fly away from the lightness of the tension. One is free to go *to* the self . . . rather than being bound *to win.*

Tension often results from a lack of integration. One does not feel "complete," or one does not feel "whole," or "ready," and therefore, one feels tension because of a sense of disunity. When the golfer walks away from his putt, he may be aware that his entire self is not concentrating on the performance; as a result, he feels at odds with himself. Without the power to concentrate, or without the feeling that everything is *pinpointed* in the attention one becomes aware that the self is not completely integrated. This awareness of the self as being disorganized in its attempt to perform gives one a sense of impending failure, and one grows more and more ill at ease as the tension builds up. The *whole* person is not tied up in the performance. Somewhere, one has lost unification, and without it, one gives less than a *total* performance. Timing suffers. Movement becomes jerky and ineffective. Rather than performing with a smoothness that comes from a sense of purpose and meaning, one performs because one *has* to. The *feel* is no longer there. In its place there is only a nagging fear of failure as all sense of meaning has temporarily been misplaced. One cannot achieve what one *wants* to achieve, for fear blocks the ability to perform as one *can* when one is relaxed.

Fear and tension in athletics does not mean one needs to learn to adjust to pressure as much as one needs to be *aware* of who one is. Once the self is accepted, there is less striving to be something one is not, and consequently, less tension. "Indeed, anxiety may take all forms and intensities, for it is the human being's basic *reaction to a danger to his existence, or to some value he identifies with his existence.*" (123, p. 35) One doesn't

144

need to strive for purpose if one has already found purpose in *being* and in existing as a unified individual while using sport as a medium for unification.

Risk in Athletics

Although death, in a realistic sense, occurs very seldom in sport, it plays a vital part symbolically. One gets "wiped out" while surfing. One gets "killed" on the tennis court. One "dies a slow death" as one tries to "kick" in track and has nothing left.

Injury for most athletes, is a form of death that is actual and a constant threat. For an injury to an athlete can *end* a career. A bad injury can cut the player off from participation altogether, or it can greatly restrict the performance. The inability to participate because of an injury throws the player into a state of nothingness—just as death does.

Have you not wondered why most players will turn and walk away from an injured individual during a game, as though the injury has not happened? Many times, it is because the athlete finds it hard to accept or to acknowledge injury or death as a personal matter because of the possibility of *finality* involved. *Tomorrow* an athlete can be eliminated by an injury, just as tomorrow a person can be eliminated by death. But one does not want to think about it *today.*

Death is one thing that an individual does not meet firsthand in life. One may know of *others* that have died, but one does not *know it oneself.* One can look upon it as it concerns *another* person, but death doesn't happen to the *living* person. Because of this, one does not think in terms of death as being a part of life; so one ignores it other than as something that will happen *once . . .* and even while thinking about this once, one thinks in terms of not being able to do anything about the *single* death experience.

Because of the seriousness of death, sport gives man an outlet because it allows man the chance to "play at death," and to laugh at it. While facing a form of death in sport, man's laughter in situations where the *potential* of death is present, allows him to mock death. Robert Jay Lifton explains this need in this way:

145

I consider the whole tone of mockery to be a very valid and important one in our time, because it reflects this loss of fit between ourselves and our symbols and between ourselves and death. What is ultimately being mocked is death, or at least the threat of various forms of absurd death. (239, p. 82)

In a way, man actually flirts with death in many sports, such as car racing; but even when someone actually gets killed, it is an *accident* and one did not actually *mean* to die during the performance. Death in all sports is an accident, just as death in life is usually an accident. One does not enter sport *expecting* to die, but one knows the *potential* is there. So relatively speaking, sport gives one a *safe* place to mock the potential of death. Yet, some sports carry a very real threat to life. In boxing, the possibility of death is a vital part of the action. "Kill the bum" are not always hollow words.

Even in high-risk sports, one ignores the reality of death in many instances because it is easier than facing it. In sports where speed is a vital factor, one rarely boasts of how close death can be if one makes an error or if the machine fails to hold up. The participant knows the potential for death is there, but he acts as if it is not.

In sports such as speed boating and car racing, the individual is constantly defying nature and the laws of nature, but during the race the individual acts as though there is no danger involved to life. The athlete seems to ignore the possibility that *he* could die. It is hard to think in terms that existence for *me* as an individual could cease in a moment. Some men are so detached from the *possibility* of their own death, that they can live with the risks involved . . . seeming to assimilate the possibility of death into their total involvement in the activity.

The striking aspect of it all, though, was not just spectacle. It was the portrait he presented, the towering physical strength and beautiful nerves under a pressure few ever feel.

This was, too, so human a thing, so movingly individualistic at a brutalizing period in history that finds men slipping deeper and deeper into the mold of mass man. . . . He was alone, and it was truly staggering to imagine the amount of hard-rock assurance he must possess in his own power and invulnerability. (109, p. 18)

One risks oneself because of the intense satisfaction one derives from the participation and the defiance of death. As Nietzsche said: "Man is a rope stretched between the animal and the Superman—a rope over an abyss." (14, p. 805a) Some choose sports with little or no risk because their concept of life will not allow them to even take the *chance* that they will be killed.

But in sport, one implies a certain amount of risk; otherwise, sport loses some of its meaning. Arnold Palmer is well loved for his willingness to risk everything as he "goes for broke." Risk adds to the *meaning,* for one is willing to sacrifice oneself in order to obtain what one desires. Gambling gives this feeling to some. "It appealed to my brinker instinct, the feeling of teetering on the brink. When you are gambling, the juices are flowing, you are really alive, really alive." (218, p. 38) "He places the bet, the juices flow, he feels really alive: action. When the bet is on, his existence is confirmed." (218, p. 39)

Some might suggest that an involvement in high-risk activities is an unconscious desire to commit suicide. Possibly it is more of an effort to continually *get away* from death rather than to escape life. Man fears what death means to his existence; therefore, by dealing directly with his fear of death by participating in high-risk sports, man feels he is in a way dealing with death. If he can overcome his fear each time out in a high speed race, he may subconsciously feel he has overcome death.

When the individual faces death, he must face what *is* in fact. He faces the possibility of *realness,* therefore, his existence becomes real. One is no longer *playing* in speed racing when the car leaves the ground and bounces over the railing. There is no time then for artificiality . . . in that moment between life and death, only what is *real* counts. One *is* when alive . . . one does not know enough about death to say the same. So one hangs onto life as long as possible for one *knows* life. Perhaps this is why so many say their life passes before them in the few moments when one is faced with the possibility of death. One looks at one's self and calculates one's worth as a *living* being. By risking death in sports, one forces oneself to look at the importance, or unimportance, of oneself. When one feels one can no longer risk the possibility that one might lose oneself accidentally, one gets out of the conflict. In describing one of his races, Mario Andretti said: "That was the hardest thing I ever did. I was all caught up, like I was defying something. It was the one time when racing seemed all so meaningless." (34, p. 42)

But to the athlete, there is another type of death other than physical death. It is the *death of potential,* either through a lack of motivation or through a subconscious desire to fail. According to the Czechoslovakian Olympic athlete Emil Zatopek,

> The qualities I like to see most in a champion are ambition, courage and will. Those are the qualities of a real man. What I dislike most is indifference, the lack of interest. That is the same thing as death. (191, p. 16)

Some never reach the heights of greatness possible simply because they aren't willing to put in the work and effort necessary to develop their skills. Others, regardless of how hard they try and how long they work, never quite make it because they *want* to fail. Bud Winter, coach of John Carlos, once described him in this way: "Our problem is that there is in Carlos what we call the will to fail. This role of underdog is so big in his book that sometimes he's afraid to get the world records because he'll no longer be the underdog." (85, p. 62) In a sense, it seems that some dare not risk *success.* Some athletes do not want to be on top because so much is expected of the winner. It is a continuous struggle to stay Number One, and once the Number One spot is lost, it is even a harder struggle to regain the pinnacle. The fun, for some, is in *getting there . . .* and when faced with the responsibilities of *being* there . . . one choses to negate the honor. One commits *potential suicide* to remain a contender rather than that of *contended for.* According to Phil Hill, "I don't think Gurney wants to win. He's a great driver but something always goes wrong and it's not always just mechanical." (34, p. 40)

Others lose as a result of various psychological hang-ups. George Frenn, who competes in the weight throw, explained that a psychotherapist told him he fouled because of a subconscious wish: "He told me that I have a self-destruction wish. That inside I don't feel that anything good should happen to me, that I feel that I don't deserve to win anything. And so I foul." (167, p. 52) Everyone who has ever coached has known an athlete who "never quite made it although he had what it took." This type athlete is afraid to *risk* his own greatness. He is afraid that even though it might be there that night, it may not hold up the *next* night, and then he would be vulnerable. He foregoes what he *is* at his best in order to eliminate the possibility that he might be *killed* on a bad night by an individual looking for an upset. He is not sure of himself or his ability, so he refuses to place himself in the limelight to be tested. He chooses to test *others,* leaving his full talents unexplored and unfulfilled. Sometimes, however, one wins in spite of oneself. In the words of Erik Van Dillen, "The day I first beat Charlie, I felt like I had done something wrong, something I wasn't supposed to. I got him on a bad day and a terrible court and I was lucky." (115, p. 29) One feels driven to make excuses for *winning,* instead of losing. One does not want to *be* that good. One does not want to be open to others who want to win big by beating the best. One does not want to be open to *success.*

Other competitors are not able to handle the guilt feelings associated with *beating* others. When one is competing, one sees the opponent as a temporary enemy seeking the same goal as oneself. To win, one must have a "killer instinct," and be able to put psychological and physical pressure on the opponent during the competition. The terminology associated with sport ("beat," "defeat," "conquer," "wipe out," etc.) suggests a criminal act rather than an ethical and sportsmanlike deed. Consequently, one loses to keep from feeling guilty. " . . . guilt is one of the major difficulties an athlete faces in competing— that to win is, in the unconscious, tantamount to destroying one's opponent." (23, p. 167) One cannot *risk* the chance that one will dislike the self by committing what seems to be an unsportsmanlike act. One must not *destroy* the opponent. It is better to turn the cheek and be destroyed oneself.

But just as some athletes mock death, and some seek a symbolic death by losing even when victory is within their potential, others do everything humanly possible to attain "eternal" life through accomplishments of such magnitude that they seem to attain immortality through their performance. We speak of the "immortal Babe Ruth." We talk about the sports figures who have become "legends," some in their own time, such as Arnold Palmer, Jonny Unitas, and Bill Russell. One becomes a hero and "lives forever" in the minds of sports fans when one's performance is such that it surpasses what most humans can do.

One does not just get *one* chance to be a hero on the sports field and to "live forever" in the record book . . . but *each* time one plays one has the chance to gain immortality. At the same time, the individual has the opportunity to be a coward, or a failure. When one plays, one chances being a hero, but one also chances being a flop.

The opportunity *to live or to die* forms its own crisis point. One often gets the chance to shoot the free throw that will win the game. Sometimes, one makes it—and the game is won. But oftentimes, one misses it . . . and *loses* the game. Keeler, an Atlanta Newspaperman who saw Bobby Jones win 13 major championships, wrote a beautiful description of how Jones carved out his immortality in the sports world:

> Looking back . . . you may see crisis after crisis where the least slip in nerve or skill or plain fortune would have spelled . . . ruin. Yet at every crisis he stood up to the shot with something which I can define only as inevitability and performed what was needed with all the certainty of a natural phenomenon. (89, p. 45)

Jones knew *who* he was and *what* he could do. He did it because he was not afraid of his own greatness. He was open to his potential, and to be less than what he was, would have been too great a risk of the vital self he possessed.

One does not always *win* during a crisis. One always *is* during a crisis if one lives an authentic life. The tremendous thing about sport is that it is only one game or one match that is won or lost. It is not the *whole package deal.* "... you can take any 10 games you want out of a guy's career and pick his record apart if that's how you want to judge him. But if you're fair, you've got to say in the end, 'The guy played 22 *years.*' " (236, p. 34)

If one goes beyond the average percentages; if one wins or loses more than the average man should win or lose ... then one either becomes known as a "pressure player," or a "choke player." One becomes tagged as a hero or as a coward because one lives *beyond the law of averages.* One chisels out a reputation by what one does *most often* during the action. But even with a reputation as a "choke" player, each time one takes the court for another game one has the *chance* to walk off as a hero ... for the performance *that* night can change the percentages.

Death makes one aware of the importance of life. William Faulkner, when accepting the 1949 Nobel Prize in Literature, said: "This is the artist's way of scribbling 'Kilroy was here' on the wall of the final and irrevocable oblivion through which he someday must pass." (239, p. 82) The athlete also leaves his mark in the best way he can ... by seeking the perfect performance, or the world record, or by performing well under extreme pressure. When faced with physical death, or when confronted with a symbolic death on the playing field, one suddenly senses how valuable life is. Risking death, regardless of how *real* death might be, makes one more aware of what one is when existing.

The athlete, like most people, ignores death because one doesn't like to think of the *end* of participation. One doesn't like the *finality* of it all. The athlete in the same light dreads getting old. Age in itself is a death, because the athlete can no longer *perform.* He is no longer a *part* of what has been his life. He can no longer participate in the thing that has allowed him recognition of his *existence.* As a result of death or old age, he is *out of it.*

One doesn't live forever ... nor can one play forever, and the athlete must face up to this fact. It is "all part of the game." *Everyone* comes under the same rules. Everyone dies. Everyone must relinquish his place, whether in life or on the sports field.

One must learn not to fear the laws of nature, for one is subject to it. When one is able to admit that death exists, one is also able to admit that life exists. There cannot be one without the other.

Death is the final defeat, but defeat any day feels like the *end* to the athlete. "I've had it," is a common expression after being beaten badly. But the athlete must risk defeat if he is to be free to reach his potential. Arnold Palmer is a hero and is loved by millions because of his ability to risk everything and to play boldly. He has not allowed himself to be restricted by victory, but he opens himself to the play of the moment. He has been willing to *chance* himself . . . as a result, he *lives* on the golf course.

> That's the way life should be lived. There's nothing more unnatural than coasting through life, bowing to left and right and accepting precious gifts. Men and football teams are the same—they both should have to reach a little. (100, p. 25)

One pays the price according to what the value system is. Some do everything possible to gain a materialistic victory. Others seek victory over themselves in preference to external victory. Either goal demands a risk.

Chapter 8

ETHICS AND MORALITY IN SPORT

How does the athlete act ethically? What is his choice when he is faced with two rights, or two "goods"? Is there any such thing as ethics and morality in sports? These are only a few questions that must be asked if one is really serious about the dynamics of sports.

Sport, in a way, has its own isolated existence and its own code of conduct. If a citizen breaks a law, he is considered to have been a harmful influence in some way to the society in which he lives. If the athlete breaks a rule on the court, he too may be punished, but in many instances the infraction of the rule is approved and encouraged by the fans, the players, and the coach. For instance, if the team needs the ball in the last few seconds, it is "good" strategy to commit a personal foul to get it. The athlete willingly and knowingly goes against the rules of the game in order to accomplish something of greater value to him—getting the ball.

Civil disobedience, which is becoming so prevalent in our country, operates on the same basis. One breaks the law willingly, and in most cases takes the punishment for the broken law, in order and in hopes of obtaining a higher value. Is this wrong? Where is the line drawn between good and bad, evil and good, right and wrong?

✳ Athletes do many irrational things within the accepted framework of sport that would force lifted brows if done outside the realm of the athletic field. In talking of his emotional, explosive personality, Ted Williams said: "I was impetuous, I was tempestuous. I blew up. I'd get so damned mad, throw bats, kick the columns in the dugout so that sparks flew, tear out the plumbing, knock out the lights, damn near kill myself. *Scream.* I'd scream out of my own frustration." (234, p. 85)

Some things would be considered to be a sign of mental

illness if done under other circumstances than pressure-filled athletics; some players slug the opponent out of anger; players have jumped off the bench and tackled the runner in a football game to prevent a long gain or a touchdown. Many build up an intense hate of the opponent before the match . . . some brood for days and weeks over lost opportunities or mistakes. But regardless of how extreme the behavior might appear to the outsider, under the scope of the rules of the game and the broad permissiveness that allows for expression of aggression and tension in sport, irrational behavior is simply termed unsportsmanlike conduct, or at its worse, unethical behavior. Many outbursts by established stars are condoned rather than punished in order to keep a winning streak going, while a lesser player might be denied the same type outbursts. It is as though one turns his head to keep from labeling behavior as it *is*.

Is athletic integrity (and, conversely, corruption) a matter of public interest? Does it matter, as appreciators of sport have so long and piously claimed it does, that games be played in an atmosphere of virtue; even righteousness? If not, what is the social utility of games—why play them at all? Drug usage, even more than speculation about bribery, college recruiting, spit-balls or TV commercials, raises such sticky questions about the fundamentals of sport that one can understand the instinctive reaction of the athletic Establishments; when it comes to drugs, they ignore, dismiss, deny. (67, p. 67)

Society regulates what is acceptable and what is not, even in the sports world, and depending on how much emphasis is placed on winning, society allows more and more leeway "under the rules," than it would if emphasis were placed on other values. For instance, in the pros it is hardly ever considered unethical to maim the quarterback, unless it is done by a "cheap shot." A "cheap shot" borders on a thin line of timing and opportunity, and whether it is in repayment for a previous "cheap shot" by the other side. So in a way, ethical behavior is relative to unethical reasoning. //

Morals and ethics are relative to the situation, and are greatly determined by the society in which we live. What is right and what is wrong differs in various locales. For instance, in some states, abortion is legal while in others it is illegal (but it is fast becoming an accepted thing throughout our country, and is therefore no longer immoral). Sport also has various moral judgements, partly because of the many different types of situations that arise within the framework of a game, and partly because of the many varied games that exist and the undefined rules connected with these games. One can beat a guy into unconsciousness in boxing, but even to attempt to hit someone in tennis is considered poor sportsmanship, to say the least. An example of how our society affects our sense of morality is the influence spectators are having on sport's events now.

> The aggression that was supposed to be ritualized and resolved in sports has burst through the frame ... simultaneously, the artificial restraints of the 19th century— playing the game, not letting the side down, being a Christian gentleman—have become open objects of derision. (196, p. 95)

It is not at all unusual to read of riots in South America where many are killed during a sporting event. In Turkey, during a soccer riot, 42 people were killed and 400 people injured. (196, p. 81) The emotions on the part of the spectators run so high, that many stadiums have built fences around the playing field to prevent fans from storming the players and officials. What at one time was accepted as sportsmanlike behavior on the part of spectators, now looks like pure white snow in comparison to the violence and disrespect shown during a sporting event. This lack of controlled behavior as a result of a change in the moral climate of our country, led Derek Sanderson (Boston Bruins' hockey player) to make this comment: "That's cool. I got fined this year for making one obscene gesture at a crowd. Tonight I had 10,000 animals making obscene gestures at me." (214, p. 67)

A newswriter spoke of Madison Square Garden fans in this way: " ... their boorishness was just one more example of an increasing trend toward bumptious audience participation in sports. The 'home advantage' . . . has been expanded to include hazards for visitors—insults, objects hurtled from the stands and even threats of bodily harm." (214, p. 67)

Who can say what factors are interacting on other factors to cause such drastic changes in ethical behavior over a period of a few years? Have the players encouraged unsportsmanlike conduct on the part of the spectators, or have the spectators influenced the players to take more liberties with the "rules of the game"? Or has it been a result of our overall lack of questioning of values and morals within our whole society? What factors led John Roche, a great basketball player, to say: "None of our guys hate any other players, but now the coaches . . . that's something different. And the fans, that's even worse . . . I'm tired of their noise. I want to beat all of their brains out—the players, the coaches and especially those people up in the seats. They're the bad ones." (103, p. 12)

Our values have changed, and so has our conduct. If one believes in *nothing more* than respect for others as a basis for moral judgements, then one would have to say that today we have immoral people living in a moral society, since our society sets the tone for what individuals consider to be right and wrong. In a way, how far one allows oneself to go in a sport in search of cultural values rather than *individual* awareness becomes a moral question. At the same time, *how* one participates also touches on moral values . . . how one sacrifices one value in preference to another . . . how one follows the "spirit of the rules," . . . how one becomes a constructive member of the society in which he lives and of which sport is a part . . . all of these things are connected with a sense of morality.

How moral one is, or how ethical one reacts to things around him in sport, deals with *specifics.* It deals with a specific point in time and a definite framework of rules. What is ethical in sport may not be ethical in society, so even though ethics and morals deal with specifics, it must also be recognized that it depends on the situation. Even the *situation* is a specific moral question. What makes hunting with a rifle sporting, and hunting with a machine gun unethical? Why is one a sportsman when he can kill a wild bird with a gun, but criminal when one shoots a bird that *belongs* to someone? If one *only* had a machine gun on a deserted island and was starving to death, would it be unethical to kill an animal with it? It depends on the *situation* one might answer. So it is with sport.

With the broadness of the boundaries of sport, one could easily choose to play unethically most of the time and still stay in the game. According to Harold McMahan, "I just lost my balance. But if it had been anything but a Tartan track I wouldn't have been caught. On other surfaces the lines aren't clearly defined." (168, p. 58) As most athletes know, there are unlimited things one can get by with if the desire is there. With this freedom of choice of how one will play the game, one moves out of the realm of isolation as an individual and becomes a being *connected* to society. As a member of what might be loosely termed the "sports society," the individual is now responsible for his relation to others, and as such must choose his own code of ethics in this light.

Sport is a personal-social phenomenon and to examine modes of meaning in the sport experience as either *only* personal or *only* social may be inadequate. In some sports, of course, there is no actual social interaction involved in performance, but there are socializing agents and models, social roles and statuses, and a pervasive social context. On one obvious level, social values and norms simply become a mode of meaning for the individual in sport. (59, p. 43)

When the basis for our value decisions depends on the meaning we find in sports, then the individual no longer attempts to "get by with what he can," but he must decide in his own mind what is the fair thing to do. If we play without being aware of any real meaning, then sports enters into a kind of limbo where any expression of human kindness is an absurdity within itself since one is there merely to survive and to win. What one decides to do with his personal freedom determines whether the athlete will enter a world of *humaneness or insensitivity* to others. What a man is *to himself* in his moral decisions determines what he will be to others in his ethical behavior.

Man finds that he really suffers through his involvement in

sport. He hurts from the training; he becomes depressed from the many defeats and losses; he risks his comfort and his security in his search for objectives that have *personal* meaning. Involvement does not mean peace and complacency. It means being open to hurt as well as to joy. If a man's involvement is an intense experience, he will lose a certain amount of peace with the self because when one *cares* deeply, one is moved within the being to look out for other living beings. The total involvement is a very *personal, intimate* relationship . . . and as such, the individual becomes involved with others on a level above the "play" factor. The caring he feels toward his sports involvement carries over to his feeling toward other individuals, and they become more than opponents or officials, or teammates. They become *living, feeling, responsive* beings . . . capable of the potential of caring and suffering as he does. Consequently, the personal, intimate feeling he has toward the play involvement becomes a close, intimate, binding relationship with others who share the same play experience. "You don't live in a world all alone. Your brothers are here too." (Albert Schweitzer on receiving the 1952 Nobel Prize) (14, p. 939b)

Most athletes never reach the level where a real sense of ethics exists in their competitive responses. Our culture has superimposed too many other values such as "win at all costs," "nice guys finish last," etc. As Derek Sanderson pointed out: "A hockey player must have three things planted in his head: hate, greed and jealousy. He must hate the other guy, he must be greedy for the puck and he must be jealous when he loses. Hockey players without those traits don't survive too long around here." (136, p. 21) The athletic field is viewed as a battlefield, not a place of reverence. "No longer are all athletes ready to treat stadiums as outdoor churches, where decorum must be maintained and everyone must be a model for the faithful in the stands." (143, p. 58) Man goes to fight and to conquer, not to follow some ethical code of conduct such as we identify with Christianity and the church. According to Gerry Philbin,

> I don't hate anybody out there, but this is a game of dog-eat-dog. It's hell. And if you don't hurt the guy in

front of you you can bet that he's going to hurt you before the game is over. You've got to be angry. If you're not the other guy will bury you. I believe in burying him before he gets the chance to throw dirt in my face. (216, p. 13)

Man seeks only to get through the game . . . not necessarily to play it to its full potential, or to *grow* through it. Yet, his finest moments are in the arena filled with tension if he can but open himself to them.

Keeping in mind that the situation in a large measure determines values for ethics, we should not demand that ethics be the same in every sport situation, any more than we should demand that ethics be the same in the United States as it is for the bushmen in Africa. What we should demand is that the ethics exhibited in sports has the same *basic nature* . . . that of respect for the rights and feelings of others, and giving the other player the same advantages you take for yourself during the game. Beyond that, ethics is determined by the sports situation.

The athlete usually recognizes the moral code in his sport. In football, it is accepted behavior that the defense will hit the opponent as hard as he can. It is *not* accepted behavior to hit a blocker from behind as hard as you can in a "clipping" action. It is also recognized that you don't send the quarterback to the sidelines with a dirty blow. But if the *other* team has just sent *your* quarterback to the sidelines by a dirty lick, then it is *right* that you take out *their* quarterback. An eye for an eye as the old saying goes. Baseball is founded on the same principle. If the pitcher brushes back a batter, then the opposing pitcher responds in the same way. Every sport has its own value system.

Decisions based on what we *like* is not necessarily a value decision. If I like baseball better than tennis, there is no moral decision in this preference (although there could be, dependent upon the reasoning behind it—if I like it because of the fact that I can get away with unfair play here and can't in tennis, then it could be a moral decision). One must determine *why* one does things to determine morality. The responsibility for these choices belongs to the man making the choice. "An ethical act . . . must be an action chosen and affirmed by the person doing it, an act which is an expression of his inward motives and attitudes." (123, p. 188)

Objectives are key factors in determining morals and ethics. When engaging in sport, the athlete is attempting to gain a certain goal, while the opponent is attempting to gain *his* goal. In this process, there is definitely a "conflict of interest" as one tries to out-think and out-maneuver the other in order to reach the goal, which commonly is summed up in the words "to win." The athlete may be able to control certain parts of the situation, but because of the human element involved, not only of self but also that of the opponent, it is impossible for him to control the total situation. He may be able to get his shot off and make a goal, but he may be unable to prevent the opponent from driving around him for an easy lay-up. When athletes compete for the same specific thing—the hockey ball, victory, etc.—there is a struggle for the objective, and competition results.

Depending upon the sport, the individual, and cultural influences, different outcomes or interests are evident. Certainly, the amateur player's reasons for competing would be quite different from that of the professional. In a sense, the amateur plays for "fun," and the professional plays for "pay." This is no longer true under our double standard where the amateur sometimes draws more money as an amateur than he could as a professional. "Coaches talk about team spirit, but I've always wondered how the hell there could be team spirit if I know that the more other linebackers screw up, the more I'll play, and the more I play, the more money I make." (249, p. 74) So, it really isn't realistic to suppose that those who make their livelihood through professional sports would be concerned with the same values as those who play only "for the fun of it." As Gary Player said: "When you're playing for money, golf is a game of sorrows." (74, p. 19) The professional athlete gears his decisions to displaying superior play in order to have a selling point for the next year's contract. Pros, in most instances, play to win and to survive, although within their own rules governed by their interests as professional athletes, there may be certain types of "ethical" play and even a form of sportsmanship defined within their role as professionals. For instance, knowing the halfback has a bum knee might motivate one player to "get him," while another might purposely avoid increasing the possibilities of further injury by not tackling low. Yet, both player's livelihoods might depend on their ability to take the halfback out of action. Even though the primary objective in a professional sport is not the development of values and a sense of humaneness, it may result from an individual's awareness of *other things* beyond obvious emphasis.

Within *true* amateur sports, where the livelihood is not involved, there is less need to base the total play on "survival," and therefore, more room for humane or sportsmanlike play. Even so, the ethical code is based on the individual's desired goal. The individual out to win at any cost would still find sportsmanship a lesser value, while the individual out to "play well" would be able to include a code of sportsmanship within the overall framework of his play.

Because of the unlimited alternatives while playing, the athlete is constantly aware that he cannot possibly take *everything* into consideration before making a decision. Knowing this, the player often experiences a feeling of uneasiness and anxiety. "Did I do right?" is a question that seems to continually lurk in the subconscious, and only when an individual *knows* he is right and is in harmony with the laws and natural forces working around him, does he know *his* life is right.

The athlete must determine his own sense of ethics when situations are not covered by rules. Does one try to "get around them," or does one play "within the rules," even when they are not clearly defined? Pushing intentionally when the referee isn't looking, taking unfair advantage of the opponent, or trying to intimidate the officials into making a wrong call are all questions of ethics.

Personal decisions are not made by someone else. They are made by *me.* The individual alone decides when to shoot, or when to attempt to block a shot, or when to push, or cheat, or argue with the official. Individual decisions are not influenced to the degree group decisions are influenced by *others.* The decision is *one's self,* so is the responsibility. What man brings into the sports action is *himself . . .* composed of past experiences, present values, and future potential. The *aloneness* of athletic participation offers the opportunity for *really* seeing the selfhood as it is. What the athlete *does* is a reflection of what the athlete *is.*

> I have no excuse for the way I acted later, for the things I did at certain sensational moments when I couldn't stand it anymore and just *reacted.* Blew up. I would probably do the same things again if the conditions were the same. That's the way I am. Even now when things are going rotten, when I'm mad about something and I wake up in the night, I'll just let off a *stream* of abuse at whatever the problem is. (236, p 33)

There is no place that one shows up as real and as authentic as one does on the athletic field. One has no time to cover up, to play a role. One reacts because of the *realness* of his reactions. What one conceives as moral and ethical shows through in action. One no longer talks about what one believes. One *lives* what one believes in the sports situation. There is a difference between ethical rules and practice of these rules. What one practices is much more authentic than what one subscribes to vocally.

One only has to look around him to know that the theory and the practice of sportsmanship have a large gap between them today.

> . . . it is in the nature of competitors to seek whatever advantage they can get. To put it bluntly, the compulsion to cheat is strong in athletes. The rules of the artificial world of sport correspond to the physical laws of the real world—they delineate the areas within which we can perform. The desire to circumvent these restrictions is a sort of Faustian impulse that in many ways can heighten sporting suspense. (69, p. 34)

We talk about sportsmanship, character, and playing the game well; yet, the actual process going on during the game is geared toward practical goals—winning, keeping the opponent from scoring, etc.—with no holds barred. What we *say* is one thing, and what we *do* during the game is something else. Many circumvent their responsibility during the heat of the battle by believing that everything involved in the action deals with ends and outcomes, not with ethics and morality. True, man's inability to be realistic at times comes from seeking the *absolute.* As humans, we have to accept the fact that "no one is perfect," yet this should not eliminate the desire to *strive* for perfection . . . or at least to strive for that point which is as close to perfection as we can come as a human being. Many men attempt to build a code of conduct on a frame of reference that might be classified as absolute morals because it results in a sense of security. If one believes that a certain thing is *so,* then to that individual it *is* so, and one does not have to question what one feels. However, without questioning, one loses the possibilities for self awareness.

Sport offers the freedom *to doubt.* One doubts his ability. One doubts his readiness. One doubts his strength. But in the doubting, one then opens himself to choices concerning *how, why,* and *what.* One who is free to question must now choose to *be* or to *pretend.* If one *fakes* it in sport, one has chosen the worse type of immorality—that of being involved in false rather than in an authentic existence. One must look for his *own* real meaning in his decision making.

The athlete must listen to what *he* is saying to himself as a person. He must open himself to what he is *feeling,* and *experiencing,* and *being* at that moment in space and time. When faced with decisions concerning values, most, through a process of rationalization, chose the solution that seems to be the greater of the two, or the more "right" of the two. The athlete usually chooses his ethical system going full speed. He does not have time to sit down and reason things out, but must make his decision during the actual movement and action. Being caught up in the action leads to many emotions, and decisions at this time cannot be completely void of what the athlete *feels.* Nor should they be. The athlete *is* what he feels. His emotions are a big part of his being. And even though he must make decisions at a time when he is highly emotionally involved, one should not discount the value of his ethical choice on the court. All men base their ethics to some degree on what they are. An ethic

Courtesy of Clear Creek High School.

based on anything outside of what the individual *actually* believes in is false. So even though the athlete may not have time for complete rationality when he must make a moral or ethical decision while going full speed, he probably has the best chance for making an *authentic* decision because of who and what he is.

After all, man is not *all* rational; therefore, one should not feel guilty when some questions must be resolved by emotions based on past experience and beliefs. Unity is the thing that one should seek, and unless one recognizes the rational *and* the emotional, this is not possible.

The *reasons* why an athlete makes a choice are often the most important part of ethics. When choices are made in the heat of the moment, the answers usually come from the truer, inner sources since this part of man is not easily touched by rationality. Therefore, reasoning under the pressure of competition is usually *what* the person is. When the reason is based on decisions made during a period of rational thought, it can be a result of what the person is, but it can also be a result of what the person hopes to gain.

One aspect of sportsmanship often emphasizes that one does not run the score up on a weaker opponent. However, if one keeps the score down to prevent one from being embarrassed in a similar situation, then it isn't done out of a sense of right and wrong (a moral decision), but as an act of practibility. But if one keeps the score "respectable" out of a sense of empathy, with no sense for future gain or reciprocation, then the act becomes an ethical act. Because the athlete and the coach are responsible for their choice, decisions become moral decisions. Without responsibility, there is no ethical question. Many lose their chance to make true moral decisions because they negate their responsibility to others.

Bobby Mitchell in talking about Paul Brown, and comparing him to Vince Lombardi: "It is a matter of belief. You believe in the man . . . you knew in advance to accept his discipline, you *wanted* his discipline. I didn't realize until later that the things I thought Paul Brown was doing *to* me he was actually doing *for* me. A player needs discipline so that he doesn't cheat." (226, p. 18)

Ethical behavior is regulated by officials in sport. Conduct outside the rules is punished immediately, while in life one does not live under such close rules and quick punishment. Because of the rules existing in sport, decisions are oftentimes a pragmatic or practical choice rather than a true ethical choice. Only in areas where there are no penalities, which comes under the "spirit of the rules," does man make a true ethical choice.

The athlete is given a sense of order and security as a result of the many known and defined rules. Outside the realm of sport, our society is not as clearly defined or structured; consequently, more confusion exists as to what is lawful and what is not. Man has always sought order in his life. The ritual and ceremony in religion has given this order to many, who may or may not understand the true meaning of religion. Sport also offers order through set rules, rituals, etc.

Even primitive people seek peace and security through rituals. But civilized man also seeks the fulfillment that comes from *understanding* things he is confronted with. As a result, he does not rely on rituals to the same extent as primitive man. With the turning away from formal religion as exemplified in the churches of today, man still seeks the order that gives his life meaning. Many find this feeling of security from organization and ritual in sport.

It has become a ritual. Before each period of a game Bobby Orr sits down in the Boston Bruins' dressing room with two hockey sticks in his hands. For the next 10 minutes or so he repeatedly lifts the sticks and lets them fall, occasionally flicking an imaginary puck into a nonexistent net. (183, p. 18)

Many rituals go on in sport, even though some are no longer needed to keep the action going smoothly. For the benefit of the TV cameras, the flipping of the coin before the game still *seems* to take place although the actual coin toss has been done before most of the fans have arrived. The list of rituals in sport is endless: the meeting of the captains before the game, the touching of the gloves of boxers before the match, the many movements of the baseball player before stepping into the box, the throwing out of the baseball by the President, the shaking of hands after the game, etc. Man finds added meaning *symbolically* through rituals. If man is ever able to find meaning *in* himself, rituals will cease to be a necessary part of his life.

The athlete many times finds that things go beyond what he understands, and what he knows should happen logically. The "great nights" come and go. In one brief moment, one can be fantastic and perform far above the highest dreams. Achievements go far beyond what one has ever done before. There are moments of glory that go beyond the human expectation, beyond the physical and emotional ability of the individual. Something *unexplainable* takes over and breathes life into the known life. One stands on the threshold of miracles that one cannot create voluntarily. The power of the moment adds up to a certain amount of religion in the performance. Call it a state of grace, or an act of faith . . . or an act of God. It is there, and the impossible becomes possible, and the last becomes first. The athlete goes beyond herself; she transcends the natural. She touches a piece of heaven and becomes the recipient of power from an unknown source.

The power goes beyond that which can be defined as physical or mental. The performance almost becomes a holy place— where a spiritual awakening seems to take place. The individual becomes swept up in the action around her—she almost *floats* through the performance, drawing on forces she has never previously been aware of.

A personal experience that stands out the most in the author's mind was the 1957 Free-Throw Championship at the National AAU Basketball Tournament. I was a freshman in college at the time, and the free-throw contest seemed like *the* height of attainment. At the time, in order to qualify one had to make at least 45 out of 50 free-throws, and then everyone who qualified shot the final night with the winner being the one who had the most out of 50. I practiced for months getting ready for the contest, and once or twice hit 50 out of 50 during practice. So I knew it was possible for me to hit a high percentage—however, being the freshman I was, I had more than a light case of nerves. Just thinking about the contest sent "butterflies" racing through my body, and the more nervous I got, the more shots I missed in practice. At the tournament, I barely got through the qualifying round (which was only watched by players attempting to qualify). I knew then that as much as I wanted to do well in the finals, that my nervousness in front of a gym full of people would result in a larger percentage of missed shots. I felt depressed because I had worked so long and hard, and I sensed that I could throw all the months of practice down the drain as a result of tension.

The night before the finals I prayed even more than usual . . . not to win, but to do well and to have a calmness within myself. I mentally went through the up-coming performance—watching the ball in my mind as it left my hands and fell through the net. I re-lived the good practice sessions when everything went smoothly, and the "touch" was there. I could mentally *feel* the motions. And then I mentally tried to practice being calm in front of the crowd, but regardless of how hard I tried—I could not get the mental image. My hands perspired as I

167

thought about it; my heart thumped loudly in my chest, and the image of missed shots kept popping back into my mind. I felt defeated . . . the feeling of defeat stayed with me as I drifted off to sleep. The thing I wanted most had proven to be beyond my will to imagine—and hopefully through the mental process, to create.

But then a strange thing happened in my sleep. Sometime during the night, I had a dream. I was shooting the free-throws, and each time the ball fell through the goal, the net would change to the image of Christ. I felt so *free* in the dream . . . it was as though *I* was flowing into the basket instead of the ball. I felt endless, unhampered. I felt a calmness that is impossible to describe. *I* was calmness, and peace, and the ball . . . and someway I was connected to the image of Christ that kept flowing from the basket. The sensation was that of transcending *everything*. I was more than I was. I was a particle flowing into *all* of life. It seems almost profane to try to describe the feeling because words are so very inadequate.

The next day, I still had the *feeling* when I awoke. I felt as though I was *floating* through the day, not just living it. That evening, when I shot my free-throws in the finals, I was probably the calmest I have ever been in my life. I didn't even see or hear the crowd. It was only me, the ball, and the basket. The number of baskets I made really had no sense of importance to me at the time. The only thing that really mattered was what I *felt*. But even so, I would have found it hard to miss even if I had wanted to. My motions were beyond my conscious control . . . the ball and I *had* to react in a certain way. It was like being on skis and going down a steep mountain. I was carried along by the force of the momentum of *whatever* I was at that time. I know now what people mean when they speak of a "state of grace." I was in a state of grace, and if it were in my power to maintain what I was experiencing at that point in time, I would have given up everything in my possession in preference to that sensation. But it was beyond my will . . . beyond my own understanding . . . beyond *me*. Yet, I was *it*.

That evening, I hit 48 out of 50 free-throws to win the 1957 Free-Throw Championship. The only thing that surprised me was the fact that two of the shots missed. I felt in such a state of perfection that it seemed only right that my performance should have been perfect. In fact, as I recall, every shot went through cleanly except the two I missed—and they rimmed the basket before dropping out. Even now, when I think of the Free-Throw Championship, I don't think about the fact that I won it . . . I think of what I *was* that evening.

This experience is something I have never shared with anyone before the writing of this book. It seemed too personal . . . too intimate. Even now, I hesitate to put it in print because of the private meaning it has to me. Yet, I feel compelled to say that I *know* there are things beyond our power to understand. I *know* God exists, regardless of the name we give Him, or the way we describe the way He works.

There have been other moments in my life where I have touched on this unlimited source of power—where things *happened* in spite of me. But never once have I been able to consciously *will* it to happen. I have been open to it because I know it's *there* . . . and I want to be a part of the complete *freeness* every chance it will have me as a part of it. But the occasions are so rare—perhaps this adds to the preciousness of it. The experience at the 1957 tournament was such an intense one, such a *transcending* one . . . that I never felt the same about winning the free-throw contest. True, I went through the motions because I was expected to defend my championship, but I no longer really *cared* about winning it. I cared about what I had experienced, and it could not be duplicated regardless of how hard I tried in the succeeding years.

But as a result of that experience, and the few ones in other situations which were similar, I do know that spirit and bodily movements can be correlated. As they intertwine, one seems to hang between the real world and another world of miracles. One accomplishes things one never dreamed of doing. One walks beyond the usual physical powers and goes *into* the power of the universe, finding streams and sensations that seem to have no beginning or end within the self. In the words of Steve Prefontaine " . . . I've never been here before. It was unexplored territory. It's strange. You find yourself in a spot of time you've never hit before and you don't know if you can finish." (251, p. 30) MacArthur Lane explained a similar sensation in this way: "Sometimes I think that the mind is just going along for the ride . . . the foot is finding its own way and the mind is just minding its own business . . . " (247, p. 25)

This feeling of *being* life, rather than just an isolated *part* of life, is probably the same feeling individuals get when they use drugs. Attaining this heightened sense of being alive without the use of drugs is probably the closest thing to *real* morality man can experience. Chip Oliver made this comment concerning the use of drugs in professional football: "They don't realize pain is strength and pleasure is weakness . . . They get carried away with alcohol and bennies instead of pulling it out of their own guts." (250, p. 53) The rightness exists in being *open* to *all* of life, while the wrongness is in denying the self-completeness by being closed to the forces regulating its existence.

Man often participates in sport while knowing little about the *why* he participates. He *believes* in it more than he *knows* about it. This is the same with religion. We have *faith* in things we do not understand. The athlete is sensitive to things that go beyond his objective measurement. The Christian is sensitive to things that go beyond his objective knowledge.

Whether man is moral or not depends on *how* and *why* he uses his potential. If one is to compete respectably in sports, one must train his body to react well during competition. One must become conditioned or fit for the sport one is engaging in. Some would say that this preparation for competition is similar to preparing for war, partly because of the emphasis placed on physical combat many centuries ago, and partly because of the emphasis placed on *survival* in our sport programs today. War and sport both exist on the premise that the most "fit" or the best prepared will win or defeat the opponent. War and peace are opposites, leading some to offer the conclusion that sport and peace are opposites; therefore, one cannot be fit and moral at the same time. This is an invalid conclusion. Morality *depends* on fitness . . . assuming that one correlates fitness with integration of the total man. In sport, man does prepare himself to participate well physically—but he also prepares himself to participate well mentally. Some do not reach both goals. Some do not reach *either* goal at times. But the fit man is at least operating on all cylinders, giving him a better than average chance of making the *right* decisions and the *right* responses. True, morality is oftentimes dependent upon the society in which we live, and decisions are often based on cultural values ... but the man who has based his life on reaching his full potential is *freer* to make his own decisions without undue influence by the society in which he lives. If one makes a just and "right" decision, whether fit or unfit, one has made a moral decision—and as such should be called a moral man.

What our culture sees in sport is the "spirit of sport," not necessarily the institutionalization of sport. Sport symbolizes what sport *means,* although meanings sometimes revert back to symbols that have no *real* meaning, but are simply custom, such as the seventh inning stretch. People identify with symbolic meanings. Even though teams may move from one location to another, the basic purpose and structure remains the same; therefore, the fan does not identify with the place or the city where the sport is held, but with the *meaning* of the team. Even when the Atlanta Hawks play in San Francisco, Atlanta fans still think of it as being *our* team. It is the same with religion, and with church members. Their church may burn and the building may be moved to another location, but it is still *their* church. They identify with the purpose and with the structure ... not with the facilities as such.

Sometimes we become too tied up with the materialistic phrases of sport (new stadiums, new physical education complexes, etc.) and forget the importance of the means and processes which go on and which give *meaning* to the activity. The *results* are not the sole answer to self-fulfilment. It is in the *becoming* or the process that holds the truth for us. We must be open to the *total* phenomenon.

Religion has the same problem at times. Some "become" religious because it offers an emotional crutch and a feeling of security. It is possible that even under these circumstances one might find *real* religion even though originally faking it, just as one might find the *real* meaning of sport while participating basically for other reasons. Even so, man's needs do not *create* religion or sport. It is *there* regardless of man's needs ... he simply discovers it. And when religion or sport become *personal* things, rather than just institutions, this is when man really begins to transcend to the truth. Sport and religion then become a part of man . . . they live not just outside of a man's life, but *inside*.

The "religious" man, on the other hand, has emerged from that tension into the tension between the world and God . . . there is no willing of one's own, but only the being joined into what is ordained; every "ought" vanishes in unconditioned being, and the world, though still existing, no longer counts. (29, p. 108)

Many miss out on what is *really* going on in sport because some parts of it stand out and cover other less conspicious aspects. We see the violence and the aggressions, but often miss the quietness in the middle of the struggle. We read about the racism, but are not aware of the moments of caring for our brothers. We see the lighted scoreboard which denotes the winners and losers, but we never know who has *actually* won within himself or herself. There is challenge, and hope, and all kinds of possibilities in sport. There is a spark that can reach the individual—that brings a certain type of holiness—of reverence when the individual listens to *more* than cultural values. Man can be serene in the midst of the action on the basketball court just as he can be serene in church. Man *is*, wherever he is.

In sport, one has numerous occasions to explore, to experiment with, and to arrive at solutions . . . to know what one doubts and why. Many, however, never recognize this opportunity, but instead become so involved in the winning and the achieving of practical goals that they miss the chance to solve the important problems such as existing in totality and in harmony with the self. Most are too worried about beating the opponent to be concerned with the *experiencing* of the self. But many times, the individual doesn't have to willingly seek sensitivity to the workings of the self to find it in sport. The involvement in sport often creates awareness whether one wants it or not. When faced with this awareness, one must learn to live with it.

Many similarities can be given between sport and religion. Each has a certain amount of ritual. Both rely on a concept of fairness (sun shines on the sinner and the saint), and both demand a total commitment. Some experiences in sport allow man to transcend himself, just as some religious experiences do. One attempts to live the *good* life in religion, which in a sense is synonymous with *performing* well in sport. One lives the religious life by seeking to do that which is *right* and just. If one fails, one seeks purification through penance and confession. Sport also depends on individuals following the rules of rightness and fairness. If one disobeys the rules, one certainly expects to be punished by the officials, just as one usually expects punishment from a Supreme Being in life.

Probably the closest similarity between sport and religion is the fact that both offer man the chance to find *wholeness* and completeness through his involvement. One finds a sense of peace in the feeling of "togetherness" in sport and in religion, just as one finds a sense of security in the rules and rituals and symbolic meanings. Some rituals in sport are so meaningful that it seems to be a religious experience. " . . . the fans began their wild chants—and the Orioles were again the puzzled outsiders at a unique religious experience." (11, p. 108)

To be moral, in sport or in religion, one must be honest with the self. One is not a Christian just because one *says* he is. One cannot vocally pay homage to one set of values while actually *believing* in another.

> . . . I am going to have to defy a couple of unwritten laws about sports. One is that above all you must be modest; you must underplay your own achievements and keep pointing out over and over again that it was your teammates who did the job. Another rule I'm going to violate is that you never make excuses. When you lose, it's always because the other team is better. They outplayed you. They were sharp and you were dull, and they deserved the victory, and all that baloney. Those two unwritten laws are responsible for more distortion and more confusion about sports than any two things I can imagine. (5, p. 40)

If one claims he plays for the fun of it when really he plays for the prestige it gives him, then this man lacks something morally. If a man claims he is something he is not, then that man is a liar and is immoral. If what one *does* on the court is what one *is*, then morality is present. Morals depend greatly on a recognition of the *real* self, with values based on the *true* being.

One might think that when one engages in sport that one no longer has to make decisions because the rules and regulations eliminate free choice. But anytime man interacts with his environment, his self, and with others, he becomes responsible for his actions. It is easy to blame other factors—the weather, the hometown spectators, another teammate—but if one shifts the blame too often, one chances losing the truth. There are times when the athlete simply plays lousy. Pete Maravich said this about himself after playing in Madison Square Garden: "I was pitiful, I was terrible, I stunk." (177, p. 25) There is no other way to get around it if one is honest. If one choses to ignore the truth and to displace the blame, then one choses to act in an immoral way. One *denies* what one is and what one has done.

Some athletes become overly absorbed in their role as a performer because the continuous action eliminates time for questions concerning their existence and their involvement in sport. These athletes *intensify* their participation because they need to *prove* something . . . to *show* someone what they can do. When one must utilize this last ounce of strength to prove something, then there is usually something lacking in the first place. If one *is*, one doesn't have to break one's back to prove it. There is a falseness to the participation when one must *play* at being a performer rather than *being* a performer.

So there are many moral and ethical questions involved in sport. Probably the most important of these is whether a man can say yes or no to who he is. He must seek his *own* rightness if he is to be moral and ethical.

Why do we play games? Why do we run and jump? Why does a man choose certain sports? Why do we stand so much pain for so few victories? Perhaps there is something in sport that adds to us *personally* that cannot be explained, and that goes far beyond our materialistic values. Perhaps it is the *realness* of our lives while involved in sport. Perhaps it is because we can't play *make believe* while caught up in the action, but we must face what *is* as it is.

To gain inner fulfilment, one must not *merely* exist, but one must exist in *completeness* . . . in *totality*. One can do this only by opening himself or herself to what is by *choice*. One must *choose* to be moral. One must *choose* to be honest. One must *choose* to be. It is only when one chooses immorality that one is immoral. Perhaps we run and jump for many reasons. Perhaps we play for many reasons. But there can be only one reason to live . . . that is to *live*. After winning at the Superbowl, Len Dawson said: "This is the ultimate; this is all there is." (60, p. 13)

EPILOGUE

I do not intend to try to summarize what has been said in this book. I only wish to make some added comments that are purely personal.

One of the things that has bothered me greatly in the last few years has been the conduct of spectators at athletic events. I think only an athlete can fully understand what it feels like to work for years to make a team—to give up things in order to be at a peak in performance—to pray that the mind and the body will be coordinated for that supreme effort that makes the difference between a good night and a poor one—and possibly only an athlete can comprehend the obscenity of having a spectator or a group of spectators be critic of the worth of years of effort when the spectator has had no real part in the agony or the glory. Somewhere, sometime, someway, the concept of sport as a ground for fair play and sportsmanship has been mutilated and changed, until today it is a concept embracing anything and everything in the name of victory. Not only are the wrong values being sought at the expense of others, but even worse, the wrong group of people are creating the change in the spirit of the game. This change is basically coming about as a result of the emotional role of spectators, and if anyone has less right to influence officials or players, it is the spectator.

For a spectator to feel he or she has the right to make a judgement concerning the quality of play on the court or the field, or to be the judge who can lessen a man's achievement through catcalls and boos, is to me one of the most depressing facets of our society today. Probably the *least* qualified individual to judge excellence is the spectator, because if he had been capable of achievement on as high a level as the competitors exhibit, he would not be a spectator, but he would be on the team competing. Possibly, this is one of the reasons so much frustration is evident in the jeers of those watching—they are incapable of the sacrifice and sweat that it takes to reach the

176

point that most athletes have reached.

In order to compete, endless hours have gone into conditioning and teamwork. But *both* sides have made sacrifices. *Both* sides have worked long hours. *Both* sides have been willing to test their skill against that of another. *Both* sides feel pain, and fatigue, and sadness, and joy. To boo or to show disrespect for a team or an individual simply because they represent another school or another organization is an offense against an individual's dignity and shows a distinct lack of understanding of the worth of achievement and dedication. Trying to kill a man psychologically or mentally is no less an act of morals than to kill an individual physically. And that *is* the intent of boos and catcalls and obscene comments by spectators and fans. Under no concept can I see this act as one of loyalty or school spirit simply because it has no place in the spirit of competiton—but even more important—because it represents total disregard to the sanctity of *being*.

It is of real credit to the decency of man that those who are more deeply involved, both physically and mentally, can display self-control and calmness at a time when pure chaos seems to be in evidence as a result of the emotional display of spectators watching a contest. Athletes do lose their tempers . . . they are lousy sports at times . . . but not nearly as often as one would expect considering the body contact, fatigue, and pressure that is being exerted on them during competition. It seems a little out of proportion to me that individuals who are directly responsible for wins or losses show greater sportsmanship and respect for opponents than those who have had no direct hand in the accomplishment.

I think sportsmanship will never improve until spectators understand the real meaning of competiton. It goes to the core of a man's life . . . to his daring to put his work on the line, to his willingness to sacrifice while knowing that sacrifices do not guarantee victory. Competition goes directly to the meaning of a man's *life*. And though the object of competition is to allow individuals to put their training and their skills on the line, the real spirit of competition includes the fact that a victory must be *earned* through individual or team effort. However, even athletes are fast losing an understanding of this vital factor in competition. They are more and more wanting something for nothing. They want security after retirement. They want pension plans, and easy hours. They ask for bonuses on the basis of what they *think* they are worth, rather than on the basis of their *proven* worth. They look to pills, and to hypnosis, and to better mechanical devices to improve performance, rather than to *themselves*. Even athletes seem to be turning their backs on the fact that everything they are seeking is *there* in the pain and the sweat and the effort, and the *personal* attempt. They go after the records and leave themselves in the locker room. They look for success and lose their potential. They work for a name, and lose their identity.

So what is it that so many sense is there, even though they may never understand it or confront it openly? Partly, it is a private scoring system that goes on within the individual. Does he have the ability to go fullspeed and to control split-second reactions? If he gets knocked down, does he have the courage to hop up and go back immediately to the action? Can he hold control over his temper and emotions when others are losing theirs and pushing the athlete to lose his? Does he have the nerve to walk on the court when the odds are 50-1 against him and still have the pride to play the game to the best of his ability? Has she got the intelligence to correct errors on the spot? Can she honestly feel respect for herself when the game is over? Can she see herself as she *is* during the real action? The list is endless. These are only a few things that are totaled up inside the athlete while the spectator and fan are watching the scoreboard for what *they* think is the result of the action.

The thing that most spectators do not understand is that the *value* is where the action is. Daring to work for the right to compete is what counts. The effort to learn self-mastery during fullspeed movements is what counts. The willingness to seek a goal when all seems beyond reach is what counts. The greatness of the human spirit in being able to go a few more minutes even though the pain of fatigue is almost inbearable is what counts. Seeking to *be* while pressure all around would force you into *unbeing* is where the value is.

And these things of value should not be profaned through signs of disrespect by those who have failed to even enter the

178

arena. Those who have not shared in the pain and the hurt and the self-sacrifice of training and of competing, have no right to share in the results. They have to earn their own score by their personal conduct as a spectator. As Chip Oliver puts it: " . . . I'd look up at the people in the stadium and realize I wasn't helping them . . . all we're doing . . . is entertaining these people, and they don't need to be entertained. They need to do their own creative thing. Deep down each of them wants to do what we're doing. But they think they can't. That's my message: they can, if they only will." (250, p. 51)

Courtesy of Brevard College. Dave Chesnut, Photographer.

Sportsmanship, or a lack of it, is really an extension of our cultural values. Arthur Ashe points out the value placed on money in sport: "People complain about our sportsmanship, but . . . with money on the line, we're trying harder than ever. If people today expect the players to be gentlemen they're looking for the wrong thing. All that counts is what goes on inside those white lines. The players will do anything to win

179

short of cheating. They want to *win*—not please people." (41, p. 13)

But even with the emphasis placed on material values, *generally* one expects another to be honest on the court as well as off the court. One expects the opponent to be courteous while playing as well as being courteous while talking over a business deal. Actions on the playing field and off of it grow out of the expectations of civilized people. One expects another to be a decent individual, whether within the confines of an athletic event or within the confines of earning a living. But, in sport, there is an area that goes beyond civilized behavior when one is open to it. On rare, beautiful moments, one goes beyond what another would expect in such a pressure-filled and trying situation. Maybe this is what we speak of when we say he "went beyond the call of duty." It is one's "duty" to be civilized, but when one can combine this with humaneness and *caring* at a point in space and time when most men would be unable to care . . . then we come to what is called the "spirit of the game." One becomes conscious of a morality beyond the rules . . . one bases his decisions on a code of conduct that includes the Christian code of conduct, "do unto others as you would have them do unto you."

This aspect of humaneness is often overlooked amid the violence and noise of competition. Many people look down on athletes as being "animals," trained to go through their paces, and to compete with the raw power found in the animal kingdom. A coach, Bud Grant, described a workout for the Minnesota Vikings in this way: "Our preparation has been animal-like. By the time the weather gets cold, an animal's fur has gotten thicker. We're the same way. We're adapting to the weather." (171, p. 44)

To consider sport as an arena of animal desires and instincts (As quoted by Press Maravich, "He's thinking, not playing basketball. He must play by instinct . . . " (173, p. 22) and nothing else, is to take away from what sport really is. Man's basic self does take part in the athletic contest—the "animal" is there—but so are the higher levels of man. He not only reacts when he plays, but he *feels*, he thinks, and perceives, and is cognitive . . . and in a sense he is reverent.

180

To believe that man is a child of God, is to believe that his body is 'a temple of God.' To be committed to that is to see the whole man—body and soul—as a unit. The care and development of the physical becomes an integral part of a man's understanding of himself.

The whole field of recreation and athletics must now be seen in a much broader context than that of won-lost records and public entertainment. (51, p. 35)

The athlete shows all the instincts of survival at times, being motivated to "kill or be killed," to protect his territory at all costs, etc., but he also shows a part of the god inside him. He goes beyond what is expected of him at times. He shows empathy for others, both friend and foe. He touches upon the golden rule at times of extreme stress and pressure, and often at the expense of himself.

> At a cross-country meet in Utah . . . Scott Bennett . . . and Brad Howes . . . were neck and neck as they came into the final stretch. Howes edged a couple of paces ahead and then suddenly stumbled and fell. Bennet stopped, helped Howes to his feet and crossed the finish line with him. Officials called it a dead heat. (252, p. 18)

The times I remember most as an athlete are unexpected joys and moments of intense *feeling* . . . being handed a small gift by a Russian player followed by the mumbled words, "You are my favorite player," riding up a mountain at two A.M. in the back of a pickup in the *rain* following a game in Mexico because we had missed the last bus, coming back from a 1-5 score in a tennis match to win it because suddenly all that mattered was me and the *ball* . . . taking a terrific fall after having my feet knocked out from under me on a rebound and realizing that I was still all together and had survived something I shouldn't have . . . going beyond the pain of a broken finger because it was more *fun* to play than to watch . . . crying because I had played so poorly, and laughing because I had played so *freely* . . . shaking all over from watching the United States flag pass by at opening ceremonies in a foreign country, and listening in awe to the Russian National anthem being played . . . joking with a Frenchman and crying with a German . . .

How can one possibly explain it all? How can you explain happiness under intolerable situations such as playing in one hundred degree heat on open courts in Peru? How can you explain *joy* in moving down court on a fast break while limping from a badly sprained ankle? How can you explain caring, and hate, and love, and honesty and cheating all in the same environment and under the same circumstances—and by the same people? How can you explain what you *feel* when you can't describe it even to yourself?

There is no way to explain it all. The only hope is to *experience* it. Only through the experience does one know it for what it is . . . *living* instead of merely existing. And with the living comes respect for other men's lives. No one has ever expressed this better than Albert Schweitzer:

Affirmation of life is the spiritual act by which man ceases to live unreflectively and begins to devote himself to his life with reverence in order to raise it to its true value . . . the man who has become a thinking being feels a compulsion to give to every will-to-live the same reverence for life that he gives to his own. He experiences that other life in his own. He accepts as being good: to preserve life, to promote life, to raise to its highest value life which is capable of development; and as being evil: to destroy life, to injure life, to repress life which is capable of development. This is the absolute, fundamental principle of the moral. . . . (246, p. 126)

BIBLIOGRAPHY

1. "Adios, Pancho," *Newsweek,* October 20, 1969, pp. 104-105.
2. Albert, Ethel M.; Denise, Theodore C., and Peterfreund, Sheldon P. *Great Traditions in Ethics.* New York: American Book Company, 1953.
3. Alcindor, Lew (With Jack Olsen), "My Story," (Part I), *Sports Illustrated*, 31:83-98, October 27, 1969.
4. Alcindor, Lew (With Jack Olsen), "A Year of Turmoil and Decision," (Part III: "My Story"), *Sports Illustrated*, 31:35-46, November 10, 1969.
5. Alcindor, Lew (With Jack Olsen), "UCLA Was a Mistake," (Part II: "My Story"), *Sports Illustrated*, 31:34-45, November 3, 1969.
6. Allen, Maury. *The Record Breakers.* Englewood Cliffs, N. J.: Prentice-Hall, Inc., 1968.
7. "Alworth Ends Retirement," *The Asheville Citizen Times*, Sunday, August 23, 1970, p. 1 (section B).
8. Andreano, Ralph. *No Joy in Mudville.* Cambridge, Mass.: Schenkman Publishing Co., 1965.
9. Angell, George, "Physical Education and the New Breed," *Journal of Health, Physical Education, and Recreation*, 40:25-28, June, 1969.
10. Annarino, Anthony, and others, "A Personal Philosophy of Physical Education," *Journal of Health, Physical Education and Recreation*, 41:24-30, 44-45, June, 1970.
11. "A Win that Couldn't Be Won," *Newsweek*, October 27, 1969, pp. 108-109B.
12. Axthelm, Pete, "A Whole New Ball Game," *Newsweek*, October 20, 1969, p. 104.
13. Bannister, R. *First Four Minutes.* New York: Dodd Mead, 1955.
14. Bartlett, John. *Bartlett's Familiar Quotations.* Boston: Little, Brown, and Company (14th Edition), 1968.
15. Berridge, Harold L., "An Experiment in the Psychology of Competition," *Research Quarterly*, 16:37-42, 1945.
16. Biddulph, Lowell G., "Athletic Achievement and the Personal and Social Adjustment of High School Boys," *Research Quarterly*, 25:1-7, 1954.
17. Blount, Roy Jr., "Lots of Stuff and No Nonsense," *Sports Illustrated*, 32:22-29, May 18, 1970.

18. Blount, Roy Jr., "The Impatience of Mrs. Job," *Sports Illustrated*, 33:24-29, August 24, 1970.
19. Bowen, Ezra, "Crossing the Bar," *Sports Illustrated*, 28:48-57, March 4, 1968.
20. Bowen, Robert, "A Man Looks at Girls' Sports," *Journal of Health, Physical Education, and Recreation*, 38:42-44, November-December, 1967.
21. Boyle, Robert H., "Big Cat on the Prowl," *Sports Illustrated*, 32:14-17, February 9, 1970.
22. Boyle, Robert H. *Sport: Mirror of American Life*. Boston: Little, Brown and Company, 1963.
23. Breisser, Arnold R. *The Madness in Sports*. New York: Appleton-Century-Crofts, 1967.
24. Britt, S. H., and James, S. Q., "Toward a Social Psychology of Human Play," *Journal of Social Psychology*, 13:351-384, 1941.
25. Browne, Evelyn, "An Ethological Theory of Play," *Journal of Health, Physical Education, and Recreation*, 39:36-39, September, 1968.
26. Brown, G. S., "A Special Brand of Fame," *Sports Illustrated*, 25:42-43, 1966.
27. Brown, Margaret C., and Sommer, Betty K. *Movement Education: Its Evolution and a Modern Approach*. Reading, Massachusetts.: Addison-Wesley, 1969.
28. Buber, Martin. *Between Man and Man*. (Translated by R. G. Smith), London: Collins, 1961.
29. Buber, Martin. *I and Thou*. (Translated by R. G. Smith. Second Edition), New York: Charles Scribner's Sons, 1958.
30. Caillois, R. *Man, Play, and Games*. Glencoe: Free Press, 1961.
31. Carry, Peter, "Caged, Tamed and On a Tear," *Sports Illustrated*, 32:28-29, May 11, 1970.
32. Caudill, W. *Effects of Social and Cultural Systems in Reactions to Stress*. Pamphlet. New York: Social Science Research Council, 1958.
33. Chapin, Kim, "El Pancho Grande," *Sports Illustrated*, 31:56-59, July 7, 1969.
34. Chapin, Kin, "Money in His Pocket, Speed in His Soul," *Sports Illustrated*, 32:38-46, May 11, 1970.
35. Cohen, T. S.; Yee W., and Brown, V., "Attitude Change and Interpersonal Attraction," *Journal of Social Psychology*, 55:207, 1961.
36. Cope, Myron, "They Cheer When the Parson is Pitching," *Sports Illustrated*, 28:72-86, May 27, 1968.
37. Cozens, Frederick, and Stumpf, Florence. *Sports and American Life*. Chicago: University of Chicago Press, 1953.
38. Cratty, Bryant J. *Movement Behavior and Motor Learning*. Philadelphia: Lea and Febiger, 1964.

39. Cratty, Bryant J. *Social Dimensions of Physical Activity*. Englewood Cliffs, N. J.: Prentice-Hall, 1967.
40. Creamer, Robert (Edited by), "Scoreboard," *Sports Illustrated*, 32:15, March, 30, 1970.
41. Creamer, Robert (Edited by), "Scoreboard," *Sports Illustrated*, 33:13, August 17, 1970.
42. "Crowd Control at Athletic Events," *Journal of Health, Physical Education, and Recreation*, 40:27-31, April, 1969.
43. Danto, Arthur C. *Nietzsche as Philosopher*. New York: MacMillan Company, 1965.
44. Deford, Frank, "Beware of the Hawks," *Sports Illustrated*, 32:22-27, April 13, 1970.
45. Deford, Frank, "East is Knicks But West is West," *Sports Illustrated*, 32:30-35, May 11, 1970.
46. Deford, Frank, "In for Two Plus the Title," *Sports Illustrated*, 32:14-17, May 18, 1970.
47. Deford, Frank, "Quitting is the Name of Any Game," *Sports Illustrated*, 30:20-21, June 30, 1969.
48. Deford, Frank, "Your Time, Not Your Dollar," *Sports Illustrated*, 30:72-83, May 12, 1969.
49. Delany, Ron, "The Running of the Green," *Sports Illustrated* (Part I), 28:18-23, January 15, 1968.
50. Delany, Ron, "How I Became A Miler: The Apprenticeship," (Part II: The Running of the Green), *Sports Illustrated*, 28:32-41, January 22, 1968.
51. Demarest, Gary W, "A Time for Courage," (R. Tait McKenzie Lecture given at 1968 AAHPER Convention), *Journal of Health, Physical Education, and Recreation*, 39:35, June, 1968.
52. Deutsch, M. "A Theory of Cooperation and Competion," *Human Relations*, 2:129-152, 1949.
53. Dewey, Robert E.; Gramlich, Francis W., and Loftsgordon, Donald (Editors). *Problems of Ethics*. New York: The Macmillan Company, 1961.
54. Eberly, Virginia D., "What the 'New Look' in Education Implies for Physical Education," *Journal of Health, Physical Education, and Recreation*, 37:28-30, September, 1966.
55. Eby, Louise Saxe. *The Quest for Moral Law*. New York: Columbia University Press, 1944.
56. Ellis, William D., "This is Our House, Y' See," *Reader's Digest*, December, 1969, pp. 65-69.
57. Erickson, E. *Childhood and Society*. (2nd Edition), New York: Norton, 1963.

185

58. Ewbank, Walter F. *Morality Without Law*. Cleveland, Ohio: World Publishing Company, 1969.
59. Felshin, Jan, "Sport and Modes of Meaning," *Journal of Health, Physical Education, and Recreation*, 40:43-44, May, 1969.
60. Ferguson, Lew, "Kansas City Fans Greet Chiefs with Open Arms," *The Asheville Citizen*, Tuesday, January 13, 1970, p. 13.
61. Frankl, Viktor E. *Man's Search for Meaning*. New York: Washington Square Press, 1963.
62. Friedman, Maurice (Editor). *The Worlds of Existentialism*. New York: Random House, 1964.
63. Fulton, R. E., "Relationship Between Teammate Status and Measures of Skill in Volleyball," *Research Quarterly*, 21:274-276, 1950.
64. Gallico, Paul. *Farewell to Sport*. New York: Alfred A. Knopf, 1938.
65. Gates, Georgia A., "An Experimental Study of the Growth of Social Perception," *Journal of Educational Psychology*, 14:449-461, 1933.
66. Gaylord, E. Curtiss. *Modern Coaching Psychology*. Dubuque, Iowa: Wm. C. Brown Book Company, 1967.
67. Gilbert, Bil, "Athletes in a Turned-On World," (Part I: Drugs in Sport) *Sports Illustrated*, 30:64-72, June 23, 1969.
68. Gilbert, Bil, "Something Extra on the Ball," (Part 2: Drugs in Sport), *Sports Illustrated*, 30:30-42, June 30, 1969.
69. Gilbert, Bil, "High Time to Make Some Rules," (Part 3: Drugs in Sport), *Sports Illustrated*, 31:30-35, July 7, 1969.
70. Gilliom, Bonnie Cherp. *Basic Movement Education for Children*. Reading, Mass.: Addison-Wesley Publishing Company, 1970.
71. Glass, Bill, "Obsessed," *Christian Athlete*, 14:14-16, January, 1970.
72. Graves, E. A., "A Study of Competitive and Cooperative Behavior by the Short Sample Technique," *Journal of Abnormal and Social Psychology*, 32:343-361, 1937.
73. Greenberg, Pearl T., "Competition in Children: An Experimental Study," *American Journal of Psychology*, 44:221-248, 1932.
74. Green, Bob, "Golf Game of Sorrows, Says Gary," *The Asheville Times*, (N. C.) Friday, April 24, 1970, p. 19.
75. Green, Richard, and Money, J., "Tomboys" and "Sissies," *Sexology*, 28: December, 1961.
76. Greenwood, Edward; Byrd, Oliver, and Rarick, Lawrence, "Psychological Values of Lifetime Sports," (Report from the Research Advisory Committee of the AAHPER Lifetime Sports Education Project), *Journal of Health, Physical Education, and Recreation*, 38: 33-37, November-December, 1967.
77. Griffith, Coleman Roberts. *Psychology and Athletics: A General Survey for Athletes and Coaches*. New York: Scribners, 1928.

78. Hand, Jack, "Pete Rozelle Testifies in Flood's Court Case," *The Asheville Citizen*, Tuesday, May 26, 1970, p. 14.
79. Harriman, Steve, "Smith Repeats National Indoor Win," *Tennis U.S.A.*, May, 1970, p. 15.
80. Herburg, Will. *The Writings of Martin Buber*. New York: The World Publishing Company, 1956.
81. Hesburgh, T. M., "The True Meaning of Sport," *Sports Illustrated*, 25:56-57, 1966.
82. Heschel, A. *Man is Not Alone*. New York: Farrar, Strauss and Young, Inc., 1951.
83. Huizinga, Johan. *Homo Ludens: A Study of the Play Element in Culture*. Boston: The Beacon Press, 1950.
84. Husman, B. F., "Aggression in Boxers and Wrestlers as Measured by Projective Techniques," *Research Quarterly*, 26:421-425, 1955.
85. "I Do What I Think is Right," *Sports Illustrated*, 30:56-62, June 9, 1969.
86. James, William. *The Will to Believe and Other Essays in Popular Philosophy*. New York: Longmans, Green, and Company, 1896.
87. Jaspers, Karl. *The Great Philosophers*. New York: Harcourt, Brace and World, 1957.
88. Jenkins, Dan, "Fancy Seeing You Here!", *Sports Illustrated*, 31:35, September 1, 1969.
89. Jenkins, Dan, "The Masters. Bobby Jones Started It All," *Sports Illustrated*, 32:44-46, April 6, 1970.
90. Jenny, John H. *Physical Education, Health Education, and Recreation: Introduction to Professional Preparation for Leadership*. New York: The Macmillan Company, 1961.
91. "Joe Kapp: Rookie Quarterback," Associated Press Release from New Orleans preceding Super Bowl. *The Asheville Times*, (N. C.) Friday, January 9, 1970, p. 14.
92. Johnson, Perry B., and others. *Physical Education: A Problem-Solving Approach to Health and Fitness*. New York: Holt, Rinehart and Winston, 1966.
93. Johnson, William, "Ararararararrgh!" *Sports Illustrated*, 30:28-33, March 3, 1969.
94. Johnson, William, "Joe Won't Be Part of the Machinery," *Sports Illustrated*, 30:22-23, June 16, 1969.
95. Johnson, William, "Triumph in Obscurity," *Sports Illustrated*, 28:68-80, April 22, 1968.
96. Jones, Robert F., "Has Anybody Here Seen Billy?" *Sports Illustrated*, 31:24-29, July 14, 1969.

97. Jones, Robert F., "The World's First Peace Pentathlon," *Sports Illustrated*, 32:50-60, May 11, 1970.

98. Jordan, Pat, "Sam of 1,000 Ways," *Sports Illustrated*, 33:36-40, August 17, 1970.

99. Kapp, Joe, with Olsen, Jack. "A Man of Machismo," (Part 1: Man of Machismo), *Sports Illustrated*, 33:26-31, July 20, 1970.

100. Kapp, Joe, with Olsen, Jack, "We Were Just a Bunch of Party Poopers," (Part 3: Man of Machismo), *Sports Illustrated*, 33:20-25, August 3, 1970.

101. Kirkpatrick, Curry, "An Answer to the Bradley Riddle," *Sports Illustrated*, 28:38-41, March 18, 1968.

102. Kirkpatrick, Curry, "It's More Fun Without Lew," *Sports Illustrated*, 32:9-11, February 2, 1970.

103. Kirkpatrick, Curry, "One More War to Go," *Sports Illustrated*, 32:12-15, March 2, 1970.

104. Kirkpatrick, Curry, "The Coed Boppers' Top Cat," *Sports Illustrated*, 28:22-27, March 4, 1968.

105. Koufax, S., "The Customers Come to Watch Us Live a Part of Our Lives," *Look*, 30:90-92, 1966.

106. Kramer, Jerry, "Death by Inches," *Sports Illustrated*, 31:50-59, August 4, 1969.

107. Kramer, Jerry. *Instant Replay*. (Edited by Dick Schaap), New York: New American Library, Inc., 1968.

108. Kram, Mark, "The Not-So-Melancholy Dane," *Sports Illustrated*, 30:79-86, April 7, 1969.

109. Kram, Mark, "The Smell of Death Was in the Air," *Sports Illustrated*, 33:18-21, July 27, 1970.

110. Kretchmar, Scott R., and Harper, William A., "Must We Have a Rational Answer to the Question Why Does Man Play?", *Journal of Health, Physical Education, and Recreation*, 40:57-58, March, 1969.

111. Lapsley, James N. (Editor). *The Concept of Willing*. Nashville, Tenn.: Abingdon Press, 1967.

112. Lawther, John D. *Psychology of Coaching*. Englewood Cliffs, N. J.: Prentice-Hall, Inc., 1951.

113. Lehman, Harvey C., and Witty, Paul C. *The Psychology of Play Activities*. New York: Barnes, 1927.

114. Lockhart, Aileene S., "The Psychology of Human Behavior Should Be a Requirement for Undergraduate Majors in Physical Education," *Journal of Health, Physical Education, and Recreation*, 38:32, June, 1967.

115. Lorge, Barry, "Van Dillen is Young Man in a Hurry," *Tennis U.S.A.*, 33:15, September, 1970.

116. Loy, John W. Jr., and Kenyon, Gerald S. (Editors) *Sport, Culture, and Society*. London: Macmillan Co., 1969.

117. Luce, R. D., and Raiffa, H. *Games and Decisions*. New York: John Wiley and Sons, Inc., 1957.

118. Maheu, René, "Sport and Culture," *International Journal of Adult and Youth Education*, 14:169-178, 1962.

119. Maslow, A. *Motivation and Personality*. New York: Harper and Brothers, 1954.

120. Maule, Tex, "A Cool Masterpiece," *Sports Illustrated*, 24:14, January 10, 1966.

121. Maule, Tex, "Kapping the Browns," *Sports Illustrated*, 32:12-16, January 12, 1970.

122. Maule, Tex, "Say It's So, Joe," *Sports Illustrated*, 30:10-15, January 20, 1969.

123. May, Rollo. *Man's Search for Himself*. New York: W. W. Norton and Co., Inc., 1967.

124. McCormick, John, "Score One for Today's Students," *Sports Illustrated*, 28:46-59, May 20, 1968.

125. McGuff, Joe, "Len Dawson: The Pride and the Passion," *Quarterback*, 1:38-42, February, 1970.

126. McPhee, John. *A Sense of Where You Are*. New York: Bantam Books, Inc., 1965.

127. Mead, Margaret. *Cooperation and Competition Among Primitive Peoples*. New York: McGraw-Hill, 1961.

128. Melnick, Merrill J., "Footballs and Flower Power," *Journal of Health, Physical Education, and Recreation,* 40:32-33, October, 1969.

129. Metheny, Eleanor. *Connotations of Movement in Sport and Dance*. Dubuque, Iowa: Wm. C. Brown Co., 1965. *ρ₁₁₄*

130. Metheny, Eleanor, "This 'Thing' Called Sport," *Journal of Health, Physical Education, and Recreation*, 40:59-60, March, 1969. ⟵

131. Miller, Daniel R., and Swanson, Guy E. *Inner Conflict and Defense*. New York: Schocken Books, 1960.

132. Mitchell C., "The Fad and Fascination of Surfing," *Holiday*, 35:122-130, 1964.

133. Moore, Robert A. *Sports and Mental Health*. Springfield, Ill.: Charles C. Thomas, 1966.

134. Morgan, William P., and others, "Fact and Fancy, or Separating Scientific Foundations from Unsupported Claims for Psychological, Sociological, and Physiological Benefits of Physical Exercise and Formal Physical Education," *Journal of Health, Physical Education, and Recreation*, 39:25-40, November-December, 1968.

135. Mudra, Darrell, "The Coach and the Learning Process," *Journal of Health, Physical Education, and Recreation*, 41:26-29, May, 1970.

136. Mulvoy, Mark and Ronberg, Gary, "The Desperate Hours," *Sports Illustrated*, 32:18-21, April 6, 1970.

189

137. Mulvoy, Mark, "Say Hey No More," *Sports Illustrated*, 26:26-29, August 7, 1967.

138. Myers, A., "Team Competition, Success, and the Adjustment of Group Members," *Journal of Abnormal and Social Psychology*, 65:325-332, 1962.

139. Myslenski, Skip, "I Do What I Think is Right," *Sports Illustrated*, 30:56-62, June 9, 1969.

140. Myslenski, Skip, "Revenge Can Be Sour," *Sports Illustrated*, 32:22-25, May 25, 1970.

141. Myslenski, Skip, "The Pressure Cooker," *Sports Illustrated*, 31:18-21, July 7, 1969.

142. Namath, Joe. *I Can't Wait Til Tomorrow, 'Cause I Get Better Looking Every Day*. New York: Random House, 1969.

143. "Namath of the Jets," *Newsweek*, September 15, 1969, pp. 57-63.

144. Nash, Jay B. *Physical Education: Interpretations and Objectives*. New York: A. S. Barnes and Company, 1948.

145. Ogilvie, Bruce and Tutko, Thomas. *Problem Athletes and How to Handle Them*. London: Pelham Books, 1966.

146. Ogilvie, Bruce C., "What is An Athlete?", *Journal of Health, Physical Education, and Recreation*, 38:48, June, 1967.

147. Olsen, Jack. *The Black Athlete, A Shameful Story*. New York: Time-Life Books, 1969.

148. Olsen, Jack, "The Black Athlete—A Shameful Story," (Part 1), *Sports Illustrated*, 29:10-27, July 1, 1968.

149. Olsen, Jack, "Pride and Prejudice," (Part 2: The Black Athlete), *Sports Illustrated*, 29:18-31, July 8, 1968.

150. Olsen, Jack, "In an Alien World," (Part 3: The Black Athlete), *Sports Illustrated*, 29:28-43, July 15, 1968.

151. Olsen, Jack, "In the Back of the Bus," (Part 4: The Black Athlete), *Sports Illustrated*, 29:28-40, July 22, 1968.

152. Olsen, Jack, "The Anguish of a Team Divided," (Part 5: The Black Athlete), *Sports Illustrated*, 29:20-35, July 29, 1968.

153. Olson, Edward C., "Individual Rights for the Coach," *Journal of Health, Physical Education, and Recreation*, 41:16, January, 1970.

154. Organ, Troy Wilson (Editor). *The Examined Life*. Boston: Houghton Mifflin Company, 1956.

155. Ottum, Bob, "Dolls on the Move to Mexico," *Sports Illustrated*, 29:16-19, September 2, 1968.

156. Ottum, Bob, "Grim Countdown to the Games," *Sports Illustrated*, 29:36-43, October 14, 1968.

157. Ottum, Bob, "Trials of An Unlonely Miler," *Sports Illustrated*, 29:16-17, October 21, 1968.

158. Pepitone, A., and Kleiner, R., "The Effects of Threat and Frustration on Group Cohesiveness," *Journal of Abnormal and Social Psychology*, 54-192-199, 1957.

159. Peterson, Harold, "Down with the Heathen," *Sports Illustrated*, 30:38-43, February 24, 1969.

160. Philip, Alice J., "Strangers and Friends as Competitors and Cooperators," *Journal of Genetic Psychology*, 57:249-258, 1940.

161. Phillips, B. N., and D'Amico, L. A., "Effects of Cooperation and Competition on the Cohesiveness of Small Face-to-Face Groups," *Journal of Educational Psychology*, 47:65-70, 1956.

162. Phillips, Richard H., "Children's Games," in *Motivations in Play, Games and Sports*. Springfield, Ill.: Charles C. Thomas, 1967, pp. 63-71.

163. Phinizy, Coles, "The Best in Any Tank, By George!", *Sports Illustrated*, 29:42-45, 1968.

164. Phinizy, Coles, "The Unbelievable Moment," *Sports Illustrated*, 29:53-61, December 23, 1968.

165. Plimpton, George, "Excuse Me, Mr. Palmer, Sir," *Sports Illustrated*, 29:88-104, October 14, 1969.

166. Plimpton, George, "Reflections in a Diary," *Sports Illustrated*, 29:41-44, December 23, 1968.

167. Putnam, Pat, "He Knows How to Throw His Weight Around," *Sports Illustrated*, 32:52-55, March 9, 1970.

168. Putnam, Pat, "These Mills Bros. are in the Record Business, Too," *Sports Illustrated*, 32:57-58, May 4, 1970.

169. "Raider's Oliver Leaves Team to Become Hippie," *The Asheville Citizen* (N. C.), Wednesday, May 13, 1970, p. 21.

170. Ralbovsky, Marty, "At Kenyon, John Rinka Scores, Thinks," *The Asheville Times*, (N. C.) Saturday, February 7, 1970, p. 9.

171. "Rams Drill in Minnesota Snow Preparing for Vikings Saturday," *New York Times*, Thursday, December 25, 1969, p. 44.

172. Rank, O. *Will Therapy; and Truth and Reality*. New York: Knopf, 1950.

173. Rappoport, Ken, " 'I Stunk,' Says Pistol Pete; NIT Crowd Doesn't Agree," *The Asheville Times*, (N. C.) Wednesday, March 18, 1970, p. 22.

174. Rathet, Mike, "Country Pays Tribute to Great Grid Coach," *The Asheville Citizen*, (N. C.) Friday, September 4, 1970, p. 19.

175. "Rebels Any Way You Cut It," *Sports Illustrated*, 30:26-27, May 19, 1969.

176. Reed, William F., "Redemption After a False Start," *Sports Illustrated*, 32:26-27, April 6, 1970.

191

177. Reed, William F., "The Upstaging of Pistol Pete," *Sports Illustrated*, 32:22-25, March 30, 1970.
178. Ress, Paul, and Brown, Gwilym S., "A Tale of Two Idols," *Sports Illustrated*, 28:22-25, March 18, 1968.
179. Riesman, David. *The Lonely Crowd*. New Haven: Yale University Press, 1950.
180. Rogin, G., "An Odd Sport . . . and an Unusual Champion," *Sports Illustrated*, 23:94-110, October 18, 1965.
181. Rogin, Gilbert, "Is Schollander a Swimmer?", *Sports Illustrated*, 28:24-34, April 1, 1968.
182. Rollins, Richard, "The Only Year of Their Lives," *Sports Illustrated*, 29:18-21, August 12, 1968.
183. Ronberg, Gary, "Tea Party for Bobby's Bruin's," *Sports Illustrated*, 32:18-21, May 4, 1970.
184. Ronberg, Gary, "To Be a Good Joe, It Takes a Hard Sell," *Sports Illustrated*, 31:12-13, July 28, 1969.
185. Rothschild, Richard. *Reality and Illusion*. New York: Harcourt, Brace and Company, 1934.
186. Russell, William F., "I'm Not Involved Anymore," *Sports Illustrated*, 31:18-19, August 4, 1969.
187. Russell, William F., "Success Is a Journey," *Sports Illustrated*, 32:80-93, June 8, 1970.
188. Ryan, Pat, "Tea and Shiners in Glassboro," *Sports Illustrated*, 29:24-25, December 9, 1968.
189. Saal, Hubert, "The Ultimate Dancer," *Newsweek*, 75:117, May 25, 1970.
190. Sage, George H. (Editor). *Sport and American Society*. Reading, Mass.: Addison-Wesley Publishing Co., 1970.
191. "Second Thoughts," (Scorecard, Edited by Robert H. Boyle), *Sports Illustrated*, 32:16, June 8, 1970.
192. Seppy, Tom, "Sports World Morns Death of Football Coach Lombardi," *The Asheville Citizen*, (N. C.) Friday, September 4, 1970, p. 19.
193. Sharman, Jackson R. *Modern Principles of Physical Education*. New York: A. S. Barnes Company, 1937.
194. Shaw, M. E., "Some Motivational Factors in Cooperation and Competition," *Journal of Personality*, 27:155-169, 1958.
195. Shecter, Leonard, "The Coming Revolt of the Athletes," *Look*, 34:43-47, July 28, 1970.
196. Sheed, Wilfrid, "This Riotous Isle," *Sports Illustrated*, 30:78-95, April 21, 1969.

197. Shoemaker, William (with Whitney Tower), "Out of the Oven and Into the Winner's Circle," *Sports Illustrated*, 32:20-25, February 2, 1970.

198. Shrake, Edwin, "A Cowboy Named Dandy Don," *Sports Illustrated*, 29:111-129, September 16, 1968.

199. Skubic, Vera, "Emotional Responses of Boys to Little League and Middle League Competition Baseball," *Research Quarterly*, 26:342-352, 1955.

200. "Slap on the Wrist," *Newsweek*, 75:48, April 13, 1970.

201. Slovenko, Ralph, and Knight, James A. (Editors). *Motivations in Play, Games and Sports*. Springfield, Ill.: Charles C. Thomas, 1967.

202. Slusher, Howard S. *Man, Sport, and Existence: A Critical Analysis*. Philadelphia: Lea and Febiger, 1967.

203. Slusher, Howard S. *Toward a Meaningful Existence*. Dubuque, Iowa: William C. Brown Company, 1964.

204. Smith, C. H., "Influence of Athletic Success and Failure on the Level of Aspiration," *Research Quarterly*, 20:196, 1949.

205. Smith, H. *Condemned to Meaning*. New York: Harper and Row, 1965.

206. "Sports as Agents of Change," *Journal of Health, Physical Education, and Recreation*, 40:35-42, April, 1969.

207. Stumpf, Florence, and Cozens, Frederick, "Some Aspects of the Role of Games, Sports, and Recreational Activities in the Culture of Modern Primitive Peoples," *Research Quarterly*, 18:198-218, 1947.

208. Sutton-Smith, B., and Rosenberg, B. G., "Manifest Anxiety and Game Preference in Children," *Child Development*, 31:515-519,

209. Tarkenton, Fran (with Jack Olsen), "Better to Scramble Than to Lose," (Part I: Quarterback on the Run), *Sports Illustrated*, 27:74-82, July 17, 1967.

210. Tarkenton, Fran (with Jack Olsen), "A Pro Rookie's Ups and Downs," (Part 2: Quarterback on the Run), *Sports Illustrated*, 27:22-27, July 24, 1967.

211. Tarkenton, Fran (with Jack Olsen), "Dear Norm: I Cannot Return," (Part 3: Quarterback on the Run), *Sports Illustrated*, 27:36-42, July 31, 1967.

212. Tarkenton, Fran (with Jack Olsen), "Always Leave Those Monsters Laughing," (Part 4: Quarterback on the Run), *Sports Illustrated*, 27:38-45, August 7, 1967.

213. "The Best in the World," *Newsweek*, 74:70-71, September 22, 1969.

214. "The Fanatics," *Newsweek*, 75:67-68, May 4, 1970.

215. "The '60s," *Newsweek*, 74:12-19, December 29, 1969.

193

216. "The Violent World of Football's Killers," *Sports Reviews 1970 Pro Football*. New York: Splended Publications, Inc., July, 1970, pp. 10-13.

217. Tournier, Paul. *The Meaning of Persons*. New York: Harper and Row, 1957.

218. Trippett, Frank, "The Suckers," *Look*, 34:34-41, May 19, 1970.

219. Trippett, Frank, "The Unending Quest for Fun," *Reader's Digest*, December 1969, pp. 62-64.

220. Tunis, John. *The American Way in Sport*. New York: Duell, Sloan and Pearce, 1958.

221. Underwood, John, "Golf's Old Man River," *Sports Illustrated*, 28:40-44, March 25, 1968.

222. Underwood, John, "No Goody Two-Shoes," *Sports Illustrated*, 30:14-23, March 10, 1969.

223. Underwood, John, "The Desperate Coach," (Part 1), *Sports Illustrated*, 31:66-76, August 25, 1969.

224. Underwood, John, "Shave off that Thing," (Part 2: The Desperate Coach), *Sports Illustrated*, 31:21-27, September 1, 1969.

225. Underwood, John, "Concessions and Lies," (Part 3: The Desperate Coach), *Sports Illustrated*, 31:29-40, September 8, 1969.

226. Underwood, John, "We're Going to Win—You Better Believe It," *Sports Illustrated*, 31:18-23, July 28, 1969.

227. Verschoth, Anita, "Fortune Smiles on this Cookie," *Sports Illustrated*, 32:48-53, June 22, 1970.

228. Ward, Stephen, "The Superior Athlete," in *Motivations Play, Games and Sports*. Springfield, Ill.: Charles C. Thomas, 1967, pp. 307-314.

229. Wayman, Agnes. *A Modern Philosophy of Physical Education*. Philadelphia: W. B. Saunders Company, 1938.

230. Webb, L. *On the Edge of the Absurd*. New York: Abingdon Press, 1965.

231. Webster, Randolph W. *Philosophy of Physical Education*. Dubuque, Iowa: Wm. C. Brown Company, 1965.

232. Weiss, Paul. *Sport: A Philosophic Inquiry*. Carbondale, Ill.: Southern Illinois Press, 1969.

233. "What Do We Believe about Physical Education for Children?" (Report from the AAHPER National Conference for College Teachers Preparing Elementary Education Majors to Teach Physical Education), *Journal of Health, Physical Education, and Recreation*, 38:12-14, May, 1967.

234. Williams, Ted (with John Underwood), "Hitting was my Life," (Part 1), *Sports Illustrated*, 28:82-105, June 10, 1968.

235. Williams, Ted (with John Underwood), "Smooth and Stormy Seasons," (Part 2: Hitting was my Life), *Sports Illustrated*, 28:30-46, June 17, 1968.

236. Williams, Ted (with John Underwood), "Teddy Ballgame Lets 'Em Have It," (Part 3: Hitting was my Life), *Sports Illustrated*, 28:28-38, June 24, 1968.

237. Williams, Ted (with John Underwood), "Last Days of Glory," (Part 4: Hitting was my Life), *Sports Illustrated*, 29:40-47, July 1, 1968.

238. Wind, Herbert Warren (Editor). *The Realm of Sport*. New York: Simon and Schuster, 1966.

239. Woodward, Kenneth L., "How America Lives with Death," *Newsweek*, 75:81-88, April 6, 1970.

240. "You Gotta Have Heart," *Newsweek*, 75:93-94, May 18, 1970.

241. Yukie, Eleanor C., "Group Movement and Growth in a Physical Education Class," *Research Quarterly*, 26:222-333, 1955.

242. Zander, A., and Curtis, T., "Effects of Social Power on Aspiration Setting and Striving," *Journal of Abnormal and Social Psychology*, 64:63-74, 1962.

243. "The Trials of a Rookie," *Newsweek*, October 5, 1970, 76:58-63.

244. Putnam, Pat, "Just Like a Green Bay Tree," *Sports Illustrated*, 31:28-29, December 1, 1969.

245. Houts, Jo Ann, "Feeling and Perception in the Sport Experience," *Journal of Health, Physical Education, and Recreation*, 41:71-72, October, 1970.

246. Schweitzer, Albert. *Out of My Life and Thought*. New York: The New American Library, 1949 (Translated by C. T. Campion).

247. Jones, Robert R., "You Learn the Art of Invisibility," *Sports Illustrated*, 33:23-25, November 16, 1970.

248. Meggyesy, Dave, "The Football Racket," *Look*, 34:66-77, November 17, 1970.

249. Meggyesy, Dave, "Sex and Racism in the NFL," *Look*, 34:65-74, December 1, 1970.

250. Newnham, Blaine, "Wow, Like Let's Really Try to Win," *Sports Illustrated*, 33:50-54, October 12, 1970.

251. Putnam, Pat, "The Freshman and the Great Guru," *Sports Illustrated*, 32:18-31, June 15, 1970.

252. Creamer, Robert (Editor), "Scorecard," *Sports Illustrated*, 33:18, November 23, 1970.

253. Maravich, Pete (With Curry Kirkpatrick), "I Want to Put on a Show," *Sports Illustrated*, 31:39-46, December 1, 1969.

P3